History of Japan

A brief history of Japan
the Land of the Rising Sun

www.dingopublishing.com

"Great Books Change Life"

Table of Contents

Introduction

The interminable history of Japan is a fascinating tale of perseverance and hardship but also of beauty, art, and triumph. Japanese culture, way of life, and other aspects of the society draw in a lot of interest from folks all over the world, and this country has become something of a focal point for many connoisseurs of popular culture. As is the case with every other country, everything Japan is today was shaped by historical events and, in Japan's case, these events frequently affected other countries and even the entire world.

Japan is also an interesting case study of how much a country's course can be affected by geographical determinism. This old island nation has, for a very long time, been physically separated from the Asian mainland, and this isolation has had a major impact on the way Japan developed as a society, country, and culture. Apart from just the physical separation, isolation has repeatedly been a matter of national and foreign policy for the Japanese, as the country has gone through prolonged periods of deliberate isolationism.

This country's long history holds most of the answers, and it can demystify many things that you may not understand about the nation. The Japanese mindset, the country's past decisions, current path, and its future are all inseparably intertwined with the country's intricate history. By the time you've acquainted yourself with Japan's past, you will likely find that many dissociated pieces of the puzzle will come together to form a clearer picture of many aspects of Japanese culture.

Taking Japanese mythology into account, Japanese history begins with a story of creation, as is the case in many other countries with a rich history. As told in the first Japanese book ever written, *Kojiki*, which dates back to 712, this story not only tells how Japan came to be but also explains the creation of heaven and earth, much like the Book of Genesis. The story is also described in the *Nihon Shoki*, another old piece of Japanese literature that was written in 720.

This mythical tale speaks of Izanagi and Izanami, a divine couple whose progeny consisted of the heavens, Earth, the Japanese islands, and much else that formed the known, comprehensible world as perceived by humans. This story, particularly as it was told in the *Kojiki*, forms the foundation of Japanese mythology and the nation's Shinto religion.

According to the *Kojiki*, much like in the Book of Genesis, there was only darkness in the beginning. And in that darkness, a yet undefined, swirling mass of what could most accurately be described as matter was present, containing *everything*. In a word, the world was chaos. As the many years came and went, particles began to move, and the lighter parts of this mass thus started to separate from the heavier, moving upward to form the heavens or Takamagahara, which translates as "the high plain of heaven." The heaviest particles were left below to form the Earth while those of intermediate mass were stuck somewhere in between and formed clouds. The lightest of the elements was light itself, which, as the *Kojiki* details, was at the "top of the Universe."

Out of this process, the first primal gods (kami) were born into the Takamagahara. The first three of these deities were Amenominakanushi, Kamimusubi, and Takamimusubi. This was the beginning of a seven-generation divine lineage. As a part of the seventh generation, the male kami Izanagi and his female counterpart Izanami came along, and these were the kami who were instructed by the older generations to provide a measure of order to the still-chaotic world below.

And thus, the divine couple found themselves situated on the Heavenly Floating Bridge above the shapeless world below, consisting of little more than open, restless ocean. The kami pair had in their possession a jeweled spear called Ama no Nuboko, bestowed upon them by the elder kami to help them in their task of creation. Unsure of how they should proceed, the kami stirred the waters with the tip of the spear, and when they pulled the spear out of the water, a single drop fell back down and formed the island of Onogoro. Izanagi and Izanami decided to make this island their home.

After many hardships and tribulations, the couple formally married and sought to produce offspring and continue their task of creating the world. In the end, the divine marriage was fruitful and, as the *Kojiki* further details, Izanami gave birth to all the Japanese islands including the smaller and main ones, Honshu, Shikoku, and Kyushu. Of course, the northern-most island of Hokkaido is also among the four main islands of Japan, but it wasn't so at the time, and the same applies to present-day Chishima and Okinawa, none of which are talked about in the *Kojiki*. In total, the divine kami couple birthed the Great Eight Islands, other smaller pieces of land, as well as many succeeding deities.

This mythical account of creation and the early literature that referred to it played a prominent role in the consolidation of Japanese identity and national conscience, paving the way for the centuries of well-documented history that was to follow. And while myths are important to every enduring nation, Japan has volumes to tell in the way of real history as well.

Chapter 1: The Paleolithic and Ancient Japan

In reality, that history began a long time before the *Kojiki* and *Nihon Shoki* were ever written. As is the case with the history of any country, the tale starts with the first people of the land. As such, a detailed account of Japan's past has to stretch up to 38,000 years ago, which is the most likely time of first human habitation on the islands.

The decisive factor in the settlement of Japanese islands was the last ice age, which ended somewhere around 20,000 years ago. To the uninitiated, you may not know much about the world except it was cold, but Earth was quite a different place at the time. Among other things, an ice age meant much larger polar ice caps, which, in turn, implied lower sea levels. As such, our planet used to have land bridges where none exist today, such as between Alaska and Russia in the Bering Strait, between Australia and New Guinea, and, of course, between Japan and mainland Asia, among other locations.

Ancient people used these pathways to cross into Australia, the Americas, Japan, and many other places where they were eventually cut off and left in isolation after the last ice age. This paved the way for these folks to evolve in their own unique ways and develop specific cultures and societies, and Japan was no exception.

Historians generally break down the history of Japan into distinct, successive periods that span from the beginning to the present day, and these periods each contain their major events, figures, and other historic landmarks defining the particular timeframe. The first and longest of these periods is simply called the Japanese Paleolithic referring to a time up until the Jomon period. These first periods are usually loosely defined, overlapping, and with their starting and ending points roughly rounded off with some variation between different historians. In general, Paleolithic Japan started with the first inhabitation of the islands somewhere around 35-38,000 years ago.

Of course, records from Paleolithic Japan are scarce, to say the least, but historians, archeologists, and other scientists have still managed to paint a fairly conclusive picture of what the islands were like. Based on limited archeological evidence in the form of leftover tools and weapons, the folks who came to Japan at the time were most likely hunter-gatherers from somewhere in the northeast of the Asian continent. These groups used stone-age hunting tools and persistence hunting to hunt down deer but also much larger animals such as mammoths. In the pursuit of these animals, the tribes eventually crossed the aforementioned land bridges and ended up in Japan, where they continued to live the same lifestyle for thousands of years.

While the early tools and weapons these new inhabitants brought with them were incredibly primitive, they became more refined over time. Toward the late Paleolithic era, the inhabitants of the Japanese islands became quite masterful stonemasons, making blade-like tools and weapons, as well as ground-stone axes.

Jomon Period

Jomon houses

The Jomon ("cord pattern") period of Japanese history begins anywhere between 14,000 and 10,000 years BCE, depending on the source, and it ends in 300 BCE. The name of this period is derived from the earthenware pottery traced back to this era, which was usually adorned with cord patterns. The hunter-gatherers carved these markings into their pottery with simple bamboo sticks, rope, and other means solely for aesthetic purposes. The introduction of pottery at this time was novel and monumental enough for the historians to mark an entire historical period by it, and some of the thousands of pottery pieces found in Japan have been proven to be the oldest in the world. In fact, these inventions were so important that some historians refer to the Paleolithic period as the pre-ceramic or "sendoki" period.

In the course of the thousands of years that came to pass, the tribes came up with various designs both in the practical and decorative sense. The patterns on the pottery became more sophisticated and elaborate, and they also experimented with different shapes. Some pots, particularly earlier ones, were very rudimentary and had pointed bottoms which helped the operator stick them into the ground under the fire and leave them stable without intervention. Flat-bottomed pots also showed up with increasing frequency throughout the period, which could imply that they were used inside huts and other rudimentary structures. Jomon pottery wasn't used just for cooking, though. Indications show the tribal folks of early Japan used pots for ceremonial, religious, and other purposes.

This is further supported by the fact that, in the late Jomon period, people were also carving out figurines and small sculptures usually made out of clay or stone, now called "dogu." Some of the figurines depict impregnated women and other symbols of fertility, clearly indicating a religious connotation as they were used for prayer. The dogu figures became very fine and sophisticated in the late parts of the period.

Despite all these novelties, the islanders were still largely hunter-gatherers for most of this period. Hunting groups became larger and more organized, however, and they didn't focus solely on persistence hunting of larger game. Fishing and gathering of various nuts and fruit gradually became one of the staples of survival. The Japanese inhabitants also domesticated the dog during this period, and they used it for hunting.

Furthermore, some of the tribes may have engaged in minor cultivation of certain herbs, but this was likely just a means of somewhat complementing other sources of food. Many tribes did construct villages, however, but they were very small and used primarily as staging areas and to spend the nighttime, and many of them were not permanent. Agriculture had not been invented yet, and the houses were very primitive, consisting of little more than a pit, a cover, and a central fireplace. These dwellings became larger toward the latter part of the period, though.

Things began to change dramatically as early as 1,000 years BCE with the introduction of rice, which most likely found its way to the islands from Korea. This introduction had a drastic impact on the consolidation of Jomon communities, which began to see the value in working and sticking together and planning ahead. Rice would eventually dominate the island people's diets, and the cultivation thereof laid the groundwork for society, as agriculture always does.

Yayoi Period

Yoshinogari Historical Park in Saga Prefecture, Japan

The Yayoi period overlaps with Jomon, generally designated as a time between 900 BCE and 250 CE. This designation wasn't always the case, and the period was seen as lasting from 300 BCE to 300 CE, but historians mostly changed this designation over time. The period got its name from an area in present-day Tokyo where archeologists discovered a form of pottery so distinct that it ended up defining a new historical period.

In accordance with the historic designation, the Yayoi period was the time when rice cultivation gradually became increasingly sophisticated and crucial to survival. This steady process took place between the time when these early Japanese first made contact with rice and the time when agriculture was in full swing, which is why the *introduction* of rice is seen as having occurred anywhere between 1,000 years BCE and 300 BCE, relative to the individual scholar. Either way, the Yayoi period was the time when this revolutionary shift took place and the people on the islands became increasingly sedentary. Early on, these folks used wetlands provided to them by nature, but, over time, they mastered irrigation techniques and were able to create their own rice fields.

Rice was far from the only major innovation that made this period so crucial. The Yayoi people of Japan also began mining and using bronze and iron to cast more advanced and durable tools and weapons of their own, instead of relying on items that found their way to the island from China or Korea. As such, the people not only found a new source of food in agriculture but they also became better hunters, improving their old ways. Instead of replacing some sources of food with rice, the Yayoi people preferred to be well-fed.

Far from being different just in appearance, the pottery of this era was vastly improved as well. The Yayoi tribes used better techniques and fired their pots at much greater temperatures than the folks of Jomon, making the pots harder and longer-lasting. The pots were more refined with smooth surfaces and fine aesthetic designs, and they continued to be used for many purposes such as cooking, storage, burial, various rituals, among other things. The quality of much of the Yayoi pottery seems to imply that their manufacture was a task left to talented and learned individuals as opposed to being made by everyone.

The Yayoi people used dwellings which were also a considerable improvement when compared to Jomon houses. The villages often resembled similar settlements in China and Korea, whose civilizations had more and more influence in Japan at that time. As opposed to living in covered pits, the Yayoi folks constructed houses with oval, earthen walls and well-supported roofs. Some of the houses were quite accommodating, going up to 1,500 square feet in size. The builders put emphasis on flood protection but also on warmth, with dedicated hearths also used for cooking. Some Yayoi villagers stored their rice and other supplies in their homes while others built dedicated storage buildings. The increasingly elaborate community structure gradually started showing signs of hierarchy. Instead of just having a loosely defined leader, small village communities now appointed chiefs, effectively turning their villages into chiefdoms, which was an important shift. In a way, these chiefs were also landowners, and sometimes they lived in the biggest houses and were in charge of a village's food supply, which made them figures of authority.

The population on the inhabited Japanese islands was already considerable, with around 200,000 as early as mid-Jomon. At this point in the Yayoi era, a big population, gathered around various chiefs and other leaders, meant that conflicts over land, food production, and everything that went along with these necessities became more pronounced. Toward the latter part of the Yayoi era, communities like chiefdoms were coming together to form alliances and confederations to fight others, and conflicts were common. These chiefdoms were starting to resemble states, leading some to refer to them as "rice kingdoms."

This is how Yamatai or Yamatai-koku came to be in the lower part of the island of Honshu, at some point between the 1st and 3rd century. Yamatai is now widely accepted as the first Japanese state. One corroborating factor   is the Chinese record of that time, which refer to Chinese travelers who visited the "country" and reported that it was ruled by Queen Himiko or the "Daughter of the Sun." In particular, she was noted as being the Priest-Queen in the "Records of the Three Kingdoms," which is an old Chinese text of that era.

Himiko was most likely a priestess, who, above all, held religious authority over her confederation, but this political entity showed the makings of a state for all intents and purposes, and clearly, a country was coming into being in Japan at that time. Records also show Queen Himiko sent some of her servants to China and exchanged

18

gifts with the neighboring country as well. In all, Queen Himiko most likely ruled between 189 and 248 CE.

Kofun Period

All of this would make Queen Himiko the de facto first ruler of Japan. On the other hand, Japanese mythology has long held that Japan's first ruler and the founder of the still-ruling imperial house was Emperor Jimmu, said to have ruled from 660 to 585 BCE. This claim has since largely been refuted, though, and it's more probable that Jimmu was the Emperor of Japan somewhere around the 7th century CE, during the Kofun period.

An archaeological site in Yoshimi-cho, Saitama Prefecture. It is a group of many sideways tombs made in the 6th - 7th centuries.

It's important to understand that the Japanese have a very strong and elaborate mythology revolving around their imperial rulers, which includes the "traditional order of succession." This order draws the entire imperial line and names every ruler since Jimmu, with specific dates of birth, reign, and death. While many of these emperors were very real, the traditional order of succession remains largely a thing of mythology and legend.

The Kofun period started with the end of Yayoi in 250 and went on until 538. As if to offer a testimonial to the growing strength of early Japanese statehood, the Kofun period was characterized by new tombs that were built for the state's rulers. Of course, tombs constructed for deceased rulers were nothing new, but those that came to be built around 250 and onward were so distinct that they gave a name to their era. Kofun tombs are essentially enormous burial mounds of various designs, sizes, and shapes. One example is the Daisen Kofun tomb of Emperor Nintoku, who is believed to have ruled in the early 5th century, located in present-day Osaka. When observed from the air, the 110-acre burial mound resembles a keyhole-shaped park and is the biggest out of many found in Japan.

Apart from these tombs, quite a few other monumental things occurred during the period. The Yamato state, or confederation of chiefdoms, was growing considerably in strength in the 5th century, then situated on the Kinai plain, in the present-day Nara Prefecture of

Japan. This locale became quite a powerhouse and drew in more and more of the neighboring chiefs and local rulers. Yamatai thus expanded into the northern part of the island of Kyushu and was situated roughly between there and Kinai. Northern parts of Honshu and especially the northernmost island of Hokkaido were far from conquered at this time, though.

As this society grew stronger, certain elites started to emerge, and these circles soon began to refer to themselves as the Yamato people or clan, essentially founding an identity that now accounts for some 98% of Japanese people who identify as ethnically Yamato. More importantly, the Yamato clan founded the first and only Japanese dynasty – the Imperial House of Japan. This fact is why Japan's imperial lineage is sometimes also referred to as the Yamato Dynasty or court. Around the early 5th century, the Yamato Japanese state was finally consolidated and headed by an Emperor in the Imperial Court, thus marking the beginning of imperial rule in Japan.

Because of these important o events, the area around the Nara Prefecture has historically been the Yamato Province, and it's also why some historians point out the Yamato period as a distinct section of Japanese history, comprised of the time between late Kofun and end of the subsequent Asuka period in 710. Furthermore, the entirety of Japan is sometimes referred to simply as Yamato in various pieces of literature.

The evolving Yamato Japanese society was also propelled forward by the introduction of writing, which helped document history effectively for the first time. With all of these important events, the early Japanese state was fairly well-established, which concluded the ancient history of Japan.

Chapter 2: Asuka – The Beginning of Classical Japan

The Asuka period, which started in 538, brought Japan into the classical era and went on until 710, which is also the year where historians generally draw the line that separates "early Japan" from the rest of history. This era was eventful and affected some important changes to the development of Japanese culture, politics, and many other layers of the young Yamato state. The name of the period is derived from the Asuka region in the vicinity of present-day Nara, where the capital is believed to have been located.

A significant novelty in the Asuka period was the introduction of Buddhism to Japan. This and other influences reached Japan from mainland Asia, where friendly ties were established with the rules in China and the Korean Peninsula. Japan already had its Shinto religion at this point, including its many gods as well as rituals that were performed by the Emperor. The influx of Buddhism marked a rise in Chinese influence on most facets of early Japanese society, which resulted in a significant evolution for Yamatai. Most of the advancements in politics, art, and other spheres that were initiated during the Kofun period were now being built upon and transformed along Chinese cultural lines.

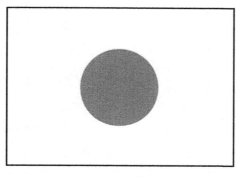

Japanese flag

Furthermore, Japan also came to be called Nihon or Nippon-koku for the first time during Asuka, changed from the previous name of Wa, given to the country by the Chinese and recorded as the first ever name for the Yamato country. This important step helped consolidate the classical Japanese state as the name of Nihon is still in use today which roughly translates to "Sun's origin" or perhaps "the place where the Sun comes from." Either way, this gave rise to the popular but informal name of the Land of the Rising Sun, sometimes the Empire of the Rising Sun. The name and the Japanese pride in it are also reflected on the country's flag.

The Rise of Shotoku Taishi

A lot of what happened during the Asuka period revolved around Prince Shotoku Taishi, who was the principal force behind many reforms and novelties at the time. The power structures in the emerging state became increasingly dependent on blood ties and intermarrying. As such, this society consisted of clans, known in Japanese as "uji," and the Yamato court was something of a playground for power play. Among the numerous clans in and around the court, the Soga clan came to prominence and distinguished itself as particularly ambitious, capable, and politically savvy. Furthermore, by this point, the Yamato society had something of a class system, where the aforementioned class was on top and involved in all manner of state and religious affairs. Beneath it was what could be described as an early working class engaging in a variety of trades and, on the very bottom, slaves.

Because of the established relations with China and Korea at that time, these countries exchanged more than just ideas with Japan. In fact, people also came from mainland Asia either to trade or to immigrate. Buddhism most likely found its way into Japan as early as the late 5th century via these established relations, though its influence in the beginning was minuscule and the faith was largely relegated to small immigrant populations that stuck with their native ways. Those in and around the Imperial Court found themselves divided on the issue, and certain clans wanted to outright suppress the foreign religion.

The divisions became even deeper toward the first half of the 6th century when the rulers from the Korean Peninsula began sending various texts and other testaments attesting to the greatness of Buddhism. Some clans became staunch opponents of this blatant influence, but the Soga clan welcomed Buddhism with open arms. This time was one of intense power play, propaganda war, but also actual war. Soon enough, the divisions over Buddhism led to open conflict and, in 587, the opposing Mononobe clan was crushed.

Just a few years later, the Soga clan assumed most of the real power in the country and effected the ascension of Empress Suiko to the throne in 593. The Empress quickly appointed Prince Shotoku Taishi as her regent, and thus began an era of strong Chinese influence and Buddhist growth. Far from being a mere puppet of foreign influence, Shotoku worked tirelessly to make the best of foreign ideas and grow the Japanese state. The Prince Regent was also personally invested in Buddhism, as he was recorded as being a Buddhist scholar and quite a sophisticated and revered one at that.

For one, Shotoku commissioned and oversaw the construction of many important Buddhist temples in Japan, some of which stand to this day, such as the Horyu-ji in the vicinity of Nara, which was built somewhere in the early 600s. Over time, Buddhism also began to somewhat fuse itself with Japanese traditions and evolve to accommodate the country's culture and other faiths. Due to Shotoku's efforts, this faith was being increasingly accepted in the country and came a long way from the marginal, unpopular idea that it once was.

Shotoku didn't just build temples and spread the good word, though. In 604, the Prince Regent constructed the so-called Seventeen Articles Constitution, though it wasn't exactly a constitution. More than anything, this document provided a set of morals to be adopted and respected by the people in order to give the Japanese society more structure and stability. Some of these seventeen articles also revolve strictly around Buddhism, instructing the observer to live by the teachings of the Buddha.

Perhaps many historians refer to this document as a constitution because it proved instrumental in the ruling clan's consolidation of power and state. In accordance with the Chinese model, the Soga rulers molded and shaped their country to become a stronger imperial state. Shotoku is also credited for having introduced a new structure to the Imperial Court through the use of ranks. The court also had to follow a certain etiquette including specific clothing items that reinforced the rank structure of the court. In the simplest terms,

Shotoku's reforms sought to shift the imperial rule and power from their hereditary ways more toward some sort of meritocracy.

Much of Shotoku's ideas of morality and honor were heavily inspired by Confucian principles from China. The rest of his articles stressed the importance of loyalty, commitment, harmony with others, and competence. The idea was to engage in a massive, state-wide effort to etch such values and ideals deep into the soul of the Japanese people and make this the foundation for future state-building and consolidation. Especially important was the adoption of these principles by the political, ruling elites. Shotoku wasn't trying to turn Japan into China by any stretch. In fact, Shotoku was a vocal critic of some aspects of the Chinese culture, and he heavily emphasized the unique culture taking form in Japan, stressing the Japanese identity as something to cherish. For all intents and purposes, all of these reforms were solely by and for the Japanese, except Shotoku and other learned men in his circles were borrowing from China's philosophies on the down low, so to speak.

The idea of Imperial Japan was starting to blossom from a seed that had been planted deep at this point. It wasn't long until the rules of Japan officially started to refer to themselves as Emperors or "tenno" in Japanese. The Imperial House of Japan was starting to gain its shape, and during this time, many crucial aspects of that ideal, which still stand today, were laid down.

Shotoku-taishi-do Hall

Furthermore, Shotoku also drew some influence from Taoism and introduced the Chinese writing system and calendar to Japan. Beyond all these social reforms, the Prince Regent also sought to improve infrastructure by improving trading roads. Historians have argued over how many of these reforms Shotoku was able to implement fully, but either way, the influence of this man was immense and had set the stage for many future developments. Shotoku's rule as a regent was perhaps the first notable time when the formal ruler or

Emperor of Japan was relegated to being little more than a symbol while real power rested elsewhere.

When Shotoku died in 622, a power vacuum was left behind, and his death set in motion a certain amount of turmoil.

The Fujiwara Takeover

Apart from the Soga clan, others also came to prominence in the early Asuka period, though many of these clans were already around during Kofun. The aforementioned Mononobe and the Nakatomi clans were particularly noteworthy during Asuka. In addition to being a form of extended family, these Japanese clans usually had a specific trade or business that they focused on. These two clans, although powerful and close to the court's power structures, were vocal opponents of Buddhism. The Nakatomi clan was prominent for its commitment to Shinto traditions and rituals, which also constituted their state duty. On the other hand, the Mononobe clan was involved in all manner of military-related trades such as armor and weapons manufacture as well as other activities, which earned them the reputation of being a military clan.

After the death of Prince Shotoku, the Soga clan continued to hold almost absolute power over the country. In a bid to curb Soga's influence and regain control for the imperial line, Prince Naka no Oe conspired with the leader of the Nakatomi clan, Nakatomi no Kamatari, to stage a coup in 645 against the Soga clan. The coup was successful, and the conspirators killed the leadership of the Soga clan and established a new government under Emperor Kotoku. The new leaders also moved the country's capital to Naniwa, which is present-day Osaka.

While the new Emperor was installed and many other changes began, the China and Buddhism-influenced reforms introduced by Shotoku remained largely intact. These changes were seen as good, and the effect they had on the strengthening of the Japanese state was undeniable. Despite the violent nature of this takeover, the standards of imperial rule established by Shotoku were thus held in high regard, including his ideals and values. Buddhism and Shintoism co-existed peacefully in Japan.

Promptly in 646, the new leadership set in motion their own changes called the Taika Reforms, and they renamed the ongoing era accordingly to Taika, meaning "Great Change." In the simplest terms, these reforms sought to make the political administration more sophisticated and efficient, but the idea was also to improve the country's infrastructure and many crucial domestic policies.

Following in the spirit of Shotoku, most of the reforms followed the Chinese model as well. To start with, the authorities needed to fund the construction of the new capital, and this required taxation. First, the government abolished the previously existing and clan-affiliated working classes. Then, the state placed all of the land in the country under its control and sought to distribute it to peasants and farmers as fairly as possible. The land reform and even the taxation system were both largely adopted from China. The taxes mostly consisted of payments in labor or military service, allowing the government to use the country's human resources for its infrastructure projects. These included the aforementioned capital, but also roads, a national military, and much more. The government now operated a bureaucracy, most of the local power-holders were integrated, and the peasant population participated in the economy. The country was becoming very sophisticated and organized.

The principal actors in the coup played a prominent role in all of this, and their personal paths were affected. Nakatomi no Kamatari was an important figure, and his power in the court grew rapidly since the coup. Once again, over time, the Emperor's power diminished to the benefit of those in his proximity. Emperor Kotoku's reign was also short-lived as he died in 654, just nine years after ascending to the throne. Empress Kogyoku took over for an even shorter reign until 661 when she too died, giving way to the rise of Nakatomi's co-conspirator, Prince Naka no Oe. This man assumed the throne as Emperor Tenji, marking the peak of his political ascension up to that point.

Tenji's rise to the throne was a desirable outcome for Nakatomi no Kamatari and his clan, as they now had an allied Emperor in power. Nakatomi's power and influence continued to grow, and he eventually changed his name to Fujiwara no Kamatari around a year before his death, founding the Fujiwara clan in 668.

The Fujiwara clan would see success after success in the centuries that followed, with their influence eventually becoming more pronounced than that of the clan they overthrew. The Fujiwara leaders used their position and connections to arrange politically crucial marriages between their daughters and the Emperors that came and went. Sons of these marriages were also frequently married to Fujiwara clan's daughters, which effectively formed a dynasty of regents through which the Fujiwara could exert control over the imperial family. The clan continued this practice and effectively ran the country until around the 11th century.

Kofukuji temple of the Fujiwara, the most powerful family clan during much of the Nara and Heian Periods.

Chapter 3: Nara Period

With the beginning of the Nara period in 710, the sometimes recognized Yamato period came to an end. Before this time, historical records are somewhat unclear when it comes to all of the capitals that may or may not have been used by the growing Japanese state. During the Nara period, however, this aspect of the country was much better recorded, and we have a very solid idea of the centers of power that were used during Nara. In fact, the capital was moved around a few times, nearly as frequently as before. For the majority of the period, the capital was located in what was then called Heijo-kyo, in present-day Nara. The move to this location was finalized in 710 and most historians view this as the first permanent capital of Japan.

By the time it ended in 794, the Nara period saw many other important events and breakthroughs that would strengthen the idea of Japan's statehood even further. Gradual changes came too, both positive and negative, some of which would resonate for centuries to come.

The Japanese implemented Chinese writing systems to an even higher degree than before using to write many important documents. Using the Chinese alphabet, the Japanese wrote the *Records of Ancient Matters*

(*Kojiki*) around 712, as well as the *Chronicles of Japan* (*Nihon Shoki*) in 720. As mentioned briefly in the introduction, these crucial pieces of literature served to clarify and consolidate the Japanese identity by giving a detailed account of the country's background and origin, both factual and mythical.

Of course, as with any old literature that contains mythical elements, quite a few stories and details were probably embellished and added to form a creative perspective. The long-term idea behind *Kojiki* and *Nihon Shoki* was far more important than their scientific merits. These books gave structure, meaning, context, and accessibility to the entire path that Japan had traveled up to that point. Other important literature was written during Nara as well, such as collections of poems like *Kaifuso* and *Man'yoshu*.

In the relatively short Nara period, Buddhist and Chinese influence in Japan continued to grow. Japanese leadership began drawing a lot of inspiration from China not just for matters of literacy and education, but also architecture, governance, lawmaking, and just the very structure of the country and culture in general.

Because of this, the government built the capital, Heijo, in Nara with a style that heavily resembled that of China's own Chang-an. The city became quite an early urban center rather quickly. Heijo had an imperial palace, residential areas, and markets, as well as main streets.

Impressively for a city at that time, estimates show Nara was home to between 100,000 and 200,000 thousand souls. Another important aspect of the city was its growing number of Buddhist temples and monasteries, which would play a major role in the latter course of this period.

In the way of governance, the Japanese idea of imperial rule carried by the Emperor (Tenno) was refined and strengthened. Although the concept of imperial rule was also influenced by China, the Japanese adjusted it to their particular needs. The meaning of "tenno," which is "heavenly emperor," perfectly illustrates the value that country's sovereigns received. The already-existing divine properties of Japan's rulers were developed further and cemented at this time. The Japanese Emperor was sovereign over the country by heavenly sanction, and the same applied to the concept of imperial succession. The Emperor's rule was incontestable,and calling it into question was an offense against divine authority.

Buddhism was quickly growing, especially in the capital, and its proponents and clergy made efforts to make it as Chinese as possible. However, while Buddhism was seeping into the corridors of power in the capital, the agriculture-driven peasant population in the country mostly stuck to the original Shinto ways of worship. The religious disconnect was only a small part of what drove the divide between the capital and the people, though. Namely, the 646 Taika Reforms initiated by Fujiwara no Kamatari and Emperor Tenji had been less than successful, especially in the realm of land and taxes.

Although the reforms granted the peasants land ownership rights, the taxes proved too hefty. The amount of rice and labor the farmers had to give to the state made farming unsustainable for many of them and, slowly but surely, growing numbers of smalltime farmers were driven to sell their land and go under the wing of wealthier landowners.

To add insult to injury, the high-ranking members of influential clans and prominent Buddhist monasteries used their positions of influence to evade taxes and, in many cases, be freed of them entirely. Needless to say, these circumstances led to a weakening of the state, with more and more powerful local landlords exercising de facto control over their areas, especially in more remote parts of the country. All of this amounted to a gradual process that eroded the government's ability to rule, and the effects were to be felt in the long term. The lack of taxes also drastically affected the country's national military force.

Despite the fact that much of the country's leaders had a way of retreating into their personal, luxurious shell, some still managed to see the proverbial writing on the wall. One such figure was the 50th Emperor himself, who ascended to the throne in 781. Emperor Kanmu was wary of the influence that the Buddhist clergy in Nara exerted in the imperial court, so he decided to move the seat of imperial power away both politically and physically. He relocated the capital and settled in the city of Nagaoka in 784. Just ten years after that, however, the capital was moved once again to Heian-kyo, present-day Kyoto, where the imperial capital would remain until 1868. And so, the Heian period began in 794.

Chapter 4: Heian Period

Between late Nara and early Heian periods, Japan had managed to expand its country into the south of Kyushu and north of Honshu islands. Breaking through these frontiers was a long-standing goal for the central government, and the breakthrough was one of the main reasons the country focused on strengthening its military. Therefore, by the time when the Heian period was underway around 802, Japan consisted of the majority of its present-day main islands, with the exception of the northernmost island of Hokkaido and perhaps the very edge of Honshu.

The Heian period was significantly longer than Nara as it lasted from 802 until around 1185, but many of the gradual, subtle changes and shifts that started during Nara carried over into the new period. Much of what happened during Heian would decide Japan's fate for centuries to come.

Throughout both Nara and Heian periods, Chinese influence is a theme to be considered. As you learned, it gained momentum and reached its height during Nara, but it continued during Heian as well. However, in the course of these centuries, the Chinese and Buddhist influence gradually decreased. This decrease didn't occur just because of Japan's Shinto religion, but also because of concerted efforts to assimilate this influence into an emerging Japanese model and culture.

Buddhism was thus gradually molded and shaped, with new sects emerging. Perhaps more importantly, however, Japan introduced the Kana syllables, which helped them form their own writing system somewhere around the 9th century. This monumental breakthrough ensured Japan would write unique literature from that point onward and slowly distance itself from China, forming a unique culture that Japan always aspired to be which also led art and literature to flourish like never before in the imperial court and among aristocrats.

The credit for this enduring contribution to Japanese development is mostly attributed to Kukai, who was a Buddhist monk and scholar who founded the Shingon Buddhist sect around 804. Shingon Buddhism remains one of the most prominent Buddhist schools of thought and practice to this day in Japan. This learned man is also recorded as being an engineer and calligrapher, among many other things, and his revision of the alphabet used in Japan was a result of interest and years of study. Of course, the introduction of Shingon, like many other sects that followed, was a major stepping stone toward making the religion more Japanese and in line with the spiritual needs of the Japanese people, doing away with Chinese influence as much as possible.

Still, The Japanese dealt with many adversities during the tumultuous Heian period the struggle to consolidate a stable state with a functional central government and foster a unified sense of nationalism was still apparent throughout the period. While all the innovations and breakthroughs were occurring in early Heian, the Asuka period's Fujiwara clan was hard at work behind the scenes, always in proximity of where power laid its head.

In the new capital of Heian, the 150-year-old Fujiwara strategy of seizing power through cleverly arranged marriages was coming to fruition more than ever. In fact, this powerful family's members in high positions in the imperial court and government were behind many of the reforms and policy changes that occurred during Nara. Apart from marrying their daughters off to Emperors, Fujiwara's power also came from its property acquisitions. Using its connections, the family would acquire land and other valuable real estate as well as manage to unburden that property of taxes.

The Fujiwara clan was not hoarding property, but using it. It would win over the favor of many other families, especially smaller and less influential ones, by transferring sizable wealth to them. However, the real power of the Fujiwara family members came from their adeptness at assuming regency for themselves.

Japan had two regency officers at that time, called the Sessho and the Kampaku. The Sessho was a regent who would rule in the name of a child Emperor until the Emperor was of age, as was the case in many other countries. The Sessho would also sometimes de facto rule on behalf of an Empress, adult or not. On the other hand, the Kampaku played a more advisory role, remaining at an acting Emperor's side. However, depending on the relation or the amount of influence a Kampaku would exert on the Emperor, he too could have been a regent and act as the ruler of the country. Between around the middle of the 9th century and the second half of the 12th century, the Fujiwara clan essentially held a monopoly on both of these offices.

The importance of securing these positions was in the aforementioned divinity of the Emperor and an absolute impossibility of deposing him without his voluntary abdication or someone arranging his death, which, if proven, would be a catastrophic offense. In many other countries, deposing a ruler and taking the throne was something that could be done in an official, legitimate manner by manipulating the legal system or engaging in other schemes, but in Japan, the throne was untouchable. This gave rise to the Fujiwara approach to conspiracy and rule from behind the curtain.

Disarray and the Rise of the Samurai

All the while, the peasantry in the countryside fell further under the control of local power brokers who, in turn, became more powerful themselves. With power and wealth came boldness and ambition, and from around the 11th century, the court in the capital was having increased difficulty in maintaining a hold on the country. The less power over the country the court had the less influence the Fujiwara family could exert as well. This clan had become incredibly adept at power play in the court, but this power came at the expense of both their ability and willingness to tend to military matters far away from Heian, especially at the chaotic and violent frontiers.

Preoccupied with a boom in the artistic expression of the era, culture, and luxuries of palace life, much of the ruling class in the capital gradually became uninterested in faraway matters of the country. Even the capital city experienced an increase in crime and anarchy at this time, so the provinces appeared completely out of reach. Wealthy influencers in the countryside noticed the anarchy. Apart from being a time of opportunity, this period was also a time of danger, as without a strong state and national army, there was nobody left to guarantee property rights or safety in general.

Out of these circumstances arose a need for security, and men of valor and violence were happy to provide for this demand. These men were proficient warriors, battle-hardened in the rough arena that was the frontier in northern Honshu. Many of them also claimed to be descendants of nobility, which, in conjunction with their adeptness at war, quickly enabled them to gather others around them and form leagues of warriors. Aware of the situation in the country, they offered their skills to those who needed security and could pay for the service. These warriors came to be known as samurai, an emerging class of fighters who adhered to the bushido code of conduct, translated and popularly known as "the way of the warrior."

Bushido refers to the entire spectrum of codes, morals, and ethics that drove the samurai lifestyle. This ethos had many Confucian elements and revolved around values such as loyalty, honor, courteous conduct, and, most importantly, discipline. The samurai were to devote themselves entirely to the *way* in war and peace alike. When they weren't fighting, the samurai were spending much of their time in the outdoors, training, perfecting their art of war. While bushido denotes the importance of honor and integrity above material gain, the samurai would frequently be rewarded by their lords with land and spoils taken in combat.

Starting as early as the 900s, powerful landowners amassed their own private armies to protect their properties but also to project power and overtake smaller clans. Soon, 1 powerful clans with armies at their backs and personal interests in their minds began to rise to prominence. The samurai were also hired by religious figures, many kinds of nobles and officials, and essentially anybody else who could afford them.

In fact, the authorities in the capital city would also hire the samurai, as they quickly became the only viable military option for anyone who needed to apply violence to remedy any situation, including the government. Powerful, militarized clans garnered massive wealth and valuable military experience through suppressing rebellions and subduing natives at the frontier. And thus, the legendary Minamoto (Genji) and Taira (Heike) clans made names for themselves. The samurai appeared at a perfectly opportune time. A strong military force was all but essential for the survival of any aspiring nation-state in the old days. And while Japan was going through its growing pains during Heian and essentially lost its military capability, the vital position of the armed forces was up for grabs. Because of this, the samurai were able to quickly rise as a warrior caste and embed themselves deeply into the state and all its affairs, which was why they would play a crucial role in Japan for centuries to come. Samurai can be sing or plural, but I just kept them plural for consistency's sake.

The Warring Clans

Already during the 10th century, the government was dealing with open rebellions by formidable clans, one of which was Taira. The government desperately needed help to maintain any semblance of order, which was a task that the court decided to outsource to the Minamoto clan. From that point on, the Minamoto clan fostered strong ties with the Fujiwara family in the capital. Both the Minamoto and the Taira clans, apart from being aristocratic, also had claims of imperial ancestry, which made their long-term goals fairly clear.

Even the divinely sanctioned throne was no longer as secure as it used to be. For a short time between the 11th and 12th centuries, a new form of rule was put in place. This new proposal was the "Insei" government, which allowed Emperors to abdicate and still influence policy while cloistered in a temple or palace despite the ruling Emperor. This type of system quickly produced conflict, notably in 1156 when two opposing Emperors, embroiled in a succession dispute, took to arms to settle their differences in a short conflict known as the Hogen Rebellion.

Amid the commotion, the Taira clan seized the opportunity to strike at the Minamoto clan, which had already embedded itself in the court's structure. Led by Taira no Kiyomori, the clan eliminated a significant portion of the Minamoto power brokers in the court, and

Kiyomori assumed a powerful regency position for himself. Much like the Fujiwara clan began doing centuries ago, the Taira clan arranged marriages, awarded important titles and wealth to its members, and intertwined itself with the imperial family. This power grab appeared to be set for success, and Kiyomori managed to produce a grandson who was a legitimate heir to the throne, assuming it in 1180 as Emperor Antoku.

Before that, however, the Minamoto clan wanted to claim revenge in 1159 when it rose up in the Heiji uprising against Taira and the central government, albeit to no avail. The Taira clan was victorious, had the Minamoto leaders banished, and proceeded to consolidate its power over the couple of decades that ensued.

Although sorely defeated, the Minamoto clan rallied its members, acquired wealth, and raised its army for war. This strong clan with substantial military experience due to the campaigns undertook for the central government over the years would not give up easily. All of these events culminated in the eruption of a decisive civil war in 1180 when Minamoto no Yoritomo led his clan into a five-year civil war to destroy the Taira family and overthrow the government.

During the war, Yoritomo's brother, the famed samurai by the name of Minamoto no Yoshitsune, would ascend to prominence and become the stuff of legends. Their father, Yoshitomo, was the man who led the foiled attempt to strike back at the Taira clan in 1159, and he was killed a year later. When Taira no Kiyomori got ahold of Yoshitomo's wife and two sons, he decided to pardon them and send the two sons their separate ways – perhaps a mistake that would come around in full swing on Taira. The two brothers wouldn't reunite until the Genpei War erupted in 1180.

Minamoto's army made significant gains quickly, seizing the east coast of Japan, which was an important strategic objective to be used as a staging area for an attack on the capital of Heian. The prevailing army finalized preparations for the siege around 1182, and the Taira leadership began to acknowledge the dire situation it was in. Before long, the clan's upper echelon evacuated the city, taking the six-year-old Emperor Antoku with them. The city was occupied by Yoshinaka, who was a cousin to the brothers, by the summer of 1183. Seizing the capital, Yoshinaka made known his ambitions of taking over the clan. While the war was still going, Yoritomo saw that he needed to act quickly and eliminate his cousin, which was a task he bestowed upon his brother Yoshitsune, where Yoritomo would distinguish himself as a great military leader.

By 1184, Yoshitsune had advanced to the rank of general, but the information on his exploits up to that point is scarce. What is known, however, is that he inflicted a crushing defeat on Yoshinaka, who sent an army to block two strategically important river crossings over the river Uji. In a pincer attack, Yoshitsune divided his army into two and destroyed the enemy at both chokepoints, after which most of Yoshinaka's men were routed. He fled Heian soon thereafter but was promptly cornered and forced to take his own life.

In the spring of 1185, the Minamoto armies caught up with the fleeing remnants of the government, the Taira clan, and their forces, and engaged them in the decisive Battle of Dan-no-ura, at the Japanese Inland Sea in the west. The imperial government was crushingly defeated and, as Japanese legends hold, the child Emperor Antoku was drowned when his grandmother descended with him into the sea to avoid capture.

After successfully routing the clan's enemies, Yoritomo ensured that all of them were eliminated both in and outside of his family. The Heian period came to an end when the Minamoto clan went back to Yoritomo's city of Kamakura and consolidated its power in 1185. This move ushered in an era where the Kamakura Shogunate was officially established in 1192, marking the beginning of a prolonged period of military rule. The warrior caste had assumed control.

Chapter 5: Kamakura and the Kenmu Restoration – Medieval Japan

The grand victory of Minamoto no Yoritomo over his rivals gave an appropriately glorious conclusion to the age of Classical Japan and, with Kamakura, Japan entered its medieval stage, often referred to as Feudal Japan. The Kamakura period would go on until 1333. This time corresponds to the rule of the first shogunate, Kamakura Shogunate until the system was abolished for a three-year period between 1333 and 1336. Some historians also hold the Kamakura period as having started from the moment when the Kamakura Shogunate was officially established some years after the Genpei War.

The Kamakura period, along with the troubles that led up to it, set the stage for an enduring struggle within the corridors of Japanese power. This struggle was to become something of an underlying theme in Japanese politics and way of life for almost the entirety of the centuries to follow, quite possibly playing a role in the events that transpired as recently as the 20th century.

The form of rule known as the Shogunate, which Yoritomo established in Kamakura in 1192, was essentially a system of military governance through dictatorship. This system also came to be known as "bakufu," which roughly translates from Japanese as "field headquarters" or "general's office." The Shogun was simply the commander of the military forces and the head of all military matters on "behalf" of the imperial government.

As such, the establishment of Yoritomo's bakufu wasn't necessarily the end of imperial rule in Japan, at least not on paper. The court, other facets of the old government, and the Emperor were neither abolished nor moved. This government remained in the capital of Heian (Kyoto), with powerful clans like Fujiwara still playing their parts in court politics, but real power moved to the countryside and resided with the Shogunate.

The Emperor still fulfilled many roles, though, although he mostly attended to ceremonial matters and acted as a symbol of the country and nation. The Emperor also played a part in religion, especially in Shintoism, as the divine ruler had been an important aspect of the cult of Shinto for centuries before this time. The Shogun was appointed and proclaimed by the Emperor, although this was a mere formality adding legitimacy to a Shogun securing his power well before this ceremonial moment. The Emperor had some control in a few areas of bureaucracy, but, in a time when sheer force was the law of the land, this power didn't amount to anything concrete. The consolidation of the emerging samurai caste, which essentially established itself as a well-defined class of the Japanese society was another change during the time. This change was somewhat intertwined with the new developments surrounding Buddhism as well. Namely, Kamakura was a time when new sects of Buddhism appeared in Japan, such as Zen Buddhism with its schools of Soto and Rinzai, which was introduced around 1191.

Zen Buddhism quickly gained great popularity within the Samurai caste, which meant that the religion also became a significant force in Japan as a whole because. Many prominent samurai served the school's interest by promoting and advocating for its teachings. The samurai were becoming the greatest cultural influencers opening many doors for the religions they favored. All the while, many Buddhist schools, including Zen, were still drawing a lot of influence and inspiration from China, adapting the teachings to the needs of Japan where appropriate.

Shogun Yoritomo died in 1199, only a few years after assuming power. Some figures in the country perhaps took this as a sign that the Shogunate was but a temporary experiment that would die with Yoritomo. A series of struggles soon began between the Kamakura Shogunate and the imperial court in the capital, culminating in the

Jokyu War, where the Shogunate defeated the government in Kyoto in 1221..

In the early 1200s, another powerful clan, called Hojo, made itself prominent and sought influence through regency in the new bakufu system. This family had been allied with Minamoto since before the downfall of the Taira clan, in which they played their parts, and they became a strong and loyal vassal to Yoritomo by this time. In fact, the connection between the two families stretched all the way back to Yoritomo's childhood.

During his exile by the Taira clan after the killing of his father, young Yoritomo was cared for by a man called Hojo Tokimasa. Once he grew up, Yoritomo married Tokimasa's daughter, and the alliance was solidified. After the Shogun's death, the Hojo clan made a series of moves during the ensuing conflicts, and the family members secured powerful positions as regents acting on behalf of not just the Emperor but also the Kamakura Shoguns. The clan also acquired a lot of land, which was invaluable capital for power building.

During their regency, the Hojo clan worked tirelessly to loosen the laws that hindered private ownership of land, transferring a lot of valuable real estate to local lords throughout the countryside. This transfer secured its loyalty, and the Hojo family, acting as the regents of the Shogunate, managed to grow a network of powerful individuals who had both wealth and warriors.

In a way, the year 1232 saw the apex of the establishment of samurai warriors as the leading caste in Japanese society with the introduction of the Joei Shikimoku legal code. This legal innovations sought to promote and often enforce much of the Confucian bushido ethos throughout the country, which embedded the samurai caste into Japanese society like never before.

A statue of Kublai Khan

The Mongol Invasions and Restoration

A period of relative stability ensued after the Hojo clan took over, but the peace was to be short-lived. The marauding Mongol forces were making gains throughout mainland Asia and, around 1259, China was subdued as well. Kublai Khan, the leader of the Mongols at that time, quickly set his sights on Japan. As history well remembers, the Mongols weren't the kind to turn down an opportunity for a good fight, so they made sure that the Shogunate knew what was coming by sending threats and demands their way. Under the guidance of the Hojo clan, all demands were promptly rejected.

The first Mongol invasion came in 1274 when the attackers tried to cross the waters and establish a foothold on the southern island of Kyushu. Tens of thousands of fierce Mongol warriors, as well as vassal fighters from the Korean peninsula, descended on Japan. The Japanese were terribly outmatched and those enemies who managed to land on Kyushu gave the defenders quite a challenge.

However, records indicate that only a small part of the invading force managed to land, so the Japanese were able to hold them off to an extent. Far from being the credit of any man wielding a sword, victory came as if from God's own hand. A typhoon struck the majority of the invading forces that were still at sea and decimated their ranks, forcing the Mongols to retreat not long into the fight.

The Mongols didn't give up, though, and they staged a new invasion in 1281. After months of fighting over the islands of Tsushima and Oki, right between Japan's Kyushu and the Korean Peninsula, the Mongols approached Japan's mainland once again, this time invading Hakata Bay in present-day Fukuoka. The Japanese were ready this time, however, and they mounted a formidable defense that led to weeks of fighting. Incredibly enough, a mighty storm swooped in once again, crushing the Mongols and forcing them back. Preoccupied with other matters in Asia, the Mongols didn't mount any future campaigns against Japan. The typhoons that saved Japan came to be called "divine winds" or kamikaze, giving rise to the word that is well-known throughout the world today.

While the defeat of the fearsome Mongols quickly became the stuff of legends, the years after the invasions weren't kind to the Kamakura Shogunate and Japan as a whole. Namely, the defense that the Japanese were able to organize during the second invasion didn't come cheap, and the Shogunate fell on hard days thereafter. The powerful local lords that the Hojo regents had amassed around them before the invasions quickly became dissatisfied when the Hojo-led Shogunate was unable to duly compensate them for their contributions to defending the country. Loyalty diminished, and Kamakura's supremacy weakened with it. Emperor Go-Daigo in Kyoto would not let this opportunity pass him by, and he devised a plan to put an end to the Shogunate once and for all in a move that would be known as the Kenmu Restoration.

The Emperor quickly obtained the support of powerful clans that had grown to despise the Hojo regents, some of which were the Ashikaga and Nitta clans. The motion to neutralize the Hojo-controlled Kamakura Shogunate was also supported by Buddhist religious figures and other high officials in the imperial court. The restoration began in 1333 and was initially a success, leaving the Hejo Shogunate regency in ruins, and Go-Daigo probably believed that a new age of true imperial rule was dawning on Japan, but he was wrong.

Chapter 6: Muromachi

The chaotic Muromachi period, sometimes called the Ashikaga period, began with the failure of the Kenmu Restoration in 1336 and would last until 1573. Instead of ushering in an era of unity and prosperity under the divine imperial rule, as Go-Daigo envisioned, the Muromachi era brought more of the same: conflict, power struggle, and more power for Shoguns. The name of the period comes from the Muromachi district of Kyoto, where the Ashikaga Shogunate was established in 1336.

The decisive factor in the failure of the Kenmu Restoration was the fact that the disdain harbored by the allied clans toward the Hojo regents was much greater than their desire to reinstate the power of the imperial court after Kamakura fell. In fact, clans, such as the family led by Ashikaga Takauji, all had great plans for their futures, and none of those plans really involved the abolishment of the very appealing concept of military dictatorship. As soon as the Hojo clan was out of the picture, Ashikaga and others started making moves.

Feudalism in Japan also grew stronger in the Muromachi period. During this time, the daimyo caste became a significant factor in the fate of the country. As the imperial hold on the country's lands was eroded further in a legal sense and more real estate became concentrated in the hands of powerful landowners, the power of local feudal lords, now generally known as daimyos, was immense.

The original idea was for the Shogun to install loyal daimyos to rule their provinces for the Shogun. Ideally, a hierarchy would be formed with the Shogun at the very top, a few hundred loyal daimyos under him, and their massive samurai armies at the bottom. Of course, in practice, this system was prone to failure. With their enormous properties, combined with the ability to use their wealth to amass armies of samurai, the daimyo would become the most powerful force in Japan.

While this period was heavily associated with upheaval and war, not everything was bad under the Ashikaga Shogunate. For a time, the economy was stabilized, and many art forms and traditions that are still popular today were introduced. The artistic concept of Japanese gardens as well as the art of flower arrangement called ikebana originated in the Muromachi period. The same goes for the Japanese tea ceremony, which is still a staple of Japanese culture. Europeans began establishing contact with Japan in the 16th century. Trade with China and the growth of domestic agriculture were further signifiers of some level of prosperity.

Nanboku-cho

Nanboku-cho or the "South and North Courts" period, as the translation suggests, is a frequently recognized sub-period that spans between 1336 and 1392, thus accounting for the first part of Muromachi, starting with the events at the end of Kenmu Restoration. The name of the sub-period is due to the fact that Japan effectively had two parallel imperial courts at this time. In 1336, Ashikaga Takauji marched into the capital and drove Emperor Go-Daigo to the south. The Emperor went to Yoshino, which was to the south of Kyoto in the present-day Nara Prefecture. Here, the defeated Emperor established his capital and proclaimed the Southern Court in 1338, the seat of legitimate imperial power. Meanwhile, the Northern Court had already been established in Kyoto around 1331, parallel to the original imperial government, owing to the Shogunate's efforts to further undermine the imperial court prior to the Kenmu Restoration. This was finalized with the official establishment of the Shogunate in Kyoto. The Northern Court had no real power, however, and was simply a legitimization of the Ashikaga Shogunate.

A struggle ensued for the rest of this sub-period, with tides turning multiple times. In fact, the Southern Court did manage to march into Kyoto on some occasions, but this was never to last. The only result was significant damage to the capital. By 1392, the Southern Court had become militarily exhausted, and the Shogunate dealt the final blow. The court in Yoshino was disbanded and the Southern Emperor, who is still recorded as having been the legitimate one, was replaced by the Northern Emperor Go-Komatsu. He was legitimized, and the system of dual imperial rule was abolished, with the new Emperor of Japan continuing to rule until 1412, under the Shogun's control, of course.

Sengoku Jidai

The Sengoku Jidai sub-period, or the Age of the Warring States, began around 1467 with the start of the Onin War. Around this time, the Ashikaga Shogunate was almost in shambles, and there was a dispute over who would become the next Shogun, which sparked the Onin War. The growth of daimyo power reached new heights by this point, and many of their clans clashed with the Shogunate during the war. By the end of the war in 1477, the capital city was severely damaged as well.

During and especially after the war, the ability of the central government in Kyoto to maintain order was essentially non-existent, as the country plunged into total disarray. Dozens if not hundreds of daimyos raised their forces and fought each other over regional supremacy. Japan de facto turned into a great number of smaller states and was simply broken up. The Ashikaga Shogunate was still standing, though, but exerting any control over the provinces was impossible.

Over the next few decades, the fighting continued. However, the more successful clan leaders gradually began to come out on top and distinguish themselves. The conflict evolved when, around 1543, the first Europeans arrived in Japan. These new arrivals were the Portuguese, and they brought various novelties to the Japanese, including firearms, such as muskets, and Christianity. Trade relations were quickly established and, given the situation in Japan, guns were more popular than Jesus. These weapons altered the course of the war, and those who could get the most guns and as fast as possible would gain the edge.

The dysfunctional and essentially useless (in its state) capital in Kyoto came in the sights of prevailing warrior clans at this point, and the Imagawa clan was the first to attempt the siege in 1560. Essentially the only obstacle in its way was the Oda clan, which was smaller but well-armed with muskets. The clan's leader, Oda Nobunaga, was a man of strategy and intelligence. His men were mostly promoted based on merit instead of birthright or class. He was also known as a ruthless samurai warrior.

*Daiun-in temple Dedicated to the warlord Oda Nobunaga
and his eldest son Nobutada*

Oda Nobunaga proceeded to crush the Imagawa clan's forces and seize Kyoto for himself in 1568. Five years later, the emerging clan hammered the last nails into the coffin of the Ashikaga Shogunate, officially ending the Muromachi military government in 1573. Oda Nobunaga entrenched himself and set the stage for the epic accomplishments of the following period of Japanese history.

The Ninja and Their Origin

Amid the chaos of this era, while the proliferation of warrior culture was reaching its peak, the illustrious ninja warriors emerged, also known (perhaps more correctly) as shinobi. During this time of political turmoil and frequent conflict among so many different interest groups, there was a growing demand for talented and meticulous individuals who could carry out special clandestine tasks for an adequate price. Sometimes, having the right man sneak into the right castle could cause more damage than a standing army at the city gates, which is a truth of warfare that stands to this day.

In the simplest possible terms, the ninja were artists of stealthy and covert action, as well as proficient in fighting and quite a few other skills. A shinobi agent could be anything from a master of a particular skill to a jack-of-all-trades who engaged in a wide range of covert operations. The ninja are known to have practiced sneaking, special weapons tactics, espionage, deception, strategy, mathematics, physical prowess, and even psychology or meteorology, among other things. This plethora of useful skills that could be practiced by a shinobi expert came to be known as ninjutsu. Therefore, the popular idea that ninjutsu is a specific martial art that was used by the ninja is a misconception. This umbrella term simply refers to the shinobi approach to the art of war.

Of course, the Sengoku period was hardly the first time someone with money came up with the idea to hire a man to spy on, sabotage, or murder his enemies under the cover of darkness. However, the ninja did see the peak of their glory during this period and made their name, while some of the earliest records of their existence date back to the earlier Muromachi.

While the fundamental idea behind being a ninja may have existed well before they actually came to light, the ninja warriors that emerged during Sengoku were fairly well-defined and unique, and their origins can be estimated to be somewhere around the 11th century.

The home ground of the shinobi in their true form has been traced to a specific locale of Iga and Koga, not far from Kyoto. While close to the capital, these areas are secluded and protected by mountainous terrain that shielded the local villages from prying eyes. The rise of the ninja most likely began with those first villages and their communities at the time, which often consisted of those who ran away from the world for one reason or another, including anyone from a nobleman who fell from grace to a common criminal. At any rate, there was a considerable level of autonomy in the region and this autonomy allowed interesting ideas to appear.

The locals began developing their own unique approaches to combat, both armed and hand-to-hand, with a lot of emphasis on stealth and covertness. Over time, there were likely "ninja families" living in those areas, eventually taking the form of clans with their own goals. The ninjutsu of these folks became more and more sophisticated possessing knowledge and learning. Generations passed on their skills and knowledge to their successors, and training also became common. Over time, these clans evolved into the shinobi that were known during Sengoku – mercenaries specializing in covert operations.

Shinobi specialists were also sometimes embedded with larger samurai forces as a wing for special operations, indeed resembling an early form of Special Forces, as we define the concept today. Some of the ninja were frowned upon by certain people because of the ways of ninjutsu, which frequently clashed with bushido principles adhered to by the regular samurai. While the way of the warrior was to do everything out in the open and apply honor to combat, the ninja lurked in the shadows. Nonetheless, shinobi tactics were frequently employed and proved indispensable, perhaps hinting at a degree of hypocrisy among some of the nobles.

As Japan moved into the Modern Era, later on, the role of the ninja was eventually phased out, at least in the form it was during Sengoku. Overall, the shinobi art of stealth and many feats were kept secret, which makes records scarce. Around the subsequent Meiji period, the ninja became quite a legend in the public eye, and even more so during the 20th century. Due to their now-prominent position in popular culture and a scarcity of verified information, the shinobi have also been the object of many misconceptions.

These misconceptions range from the idea that a ninja had to be of noble ancestry to them having superhuman abilities. The shinobi were simply people who perfected a certain trade primarily to make money, and they came from various backgrounds. There are also misconceptions about some of their weapons, like the throwing stars, or shuriken. Namely, these weapons were invented and used by the samurai for a long time, and they weren't invented by or reserved for the shinobi warriors. Black clothes with masks were also not always the case. Certainly, many shinobi did wear masks and dark clothes in order to conceal themselves on assignments, but others performed jobs that didn't require this. Unsurprisingly, there are also no records of any ninja disappearing in a cloud of smoke, although they did often master the use of explosives, poisonous gas, and many other unconventional weapons suitable for sabotage.

Chapter 7: Azuchi-Momoyama

Despite the fall of the Shogunate in Muromachi, Japan was still in a state of clan warfare. Important work still needed to be done by the emerging victors, and the Sengoku sub-period of disarray would go on until around 1600. The Azuchi-Momoyama period was a short but crucial one bringing a century of instability to an end, reestablishing Japan, and preparing it for a whole new era that fed directly into the country we know today.

The period officially started either in 1568 or 1573, depending on the historian's preference, as both the capture of Kyoto by Oda Nobunaga and the fall of the Ashikaga Shogunate were monumental events of equal magnitude. The name of the period comes from the castles where the clans of Oda Nobunaga and his most trusted general Toyotomi Hideyoshi were based, called Azuchi and Momoyama respectively. The period, ending in 1600, was a time of legendary feats and unification, as well as the last period of Feudal Japan.

Mausoleum of Lord Nobunaga ODA:

The site of Nino-maru of the Azuchi-jo castle ruins

Between the time when he took Kyoto and the fall of the Ashikaga Shogunate, Oda Nobunaga quickly began to fulfill his ambition to unify the entirety of Japan and assume control. At that time, some of his most prominent opponents included some Buddhist sects and powerful eastern clans such as Takeda and Uesugi, who certainly had the potential to foil his plans. As fate would have it, however, the leaders of both clans died before it ever came to arms between them and Nobunaga.

Once again employing his ruthlessness and modern weaponry, Nobunaga seized the opportunity and struck the Takeda clan, dealing

71

devastating blows in 1575 and destroying its dominion by 1582, after which its lands were put under his flag. Apart from guns, religion, and innovative appliances, the Europeans brought with them other military innovations, including tactics, many of which Nobunaga readily adopted to great fruition.

Nobunaga continued his quest and managed to conquer a significant part of the country by 1582, putting those lands and the daimyos that controlled them under his own administration. Unfortunately, this was to be the last year Nobunaga would spend on the battlefield. While he was en route to assist Hideyoshi's campaign in a remote part of the country, Nobunaga briefly stopped in Kyoto with only a limited personal security detail. This mistake was fatal , as he was betrayed and attacked by Akechi Mitsuhide, a disgruntled, higher-echelon general of Nobunaga's. Forced into a corner, Nobunaga committed suicide to avoid capture.

Upon hearing the dreadful news, Toyotomi Hideyoshi quickly gathered his forces and went back to Kyoto, putting his campaigns on hold to attend to these urgent matters. Just days later, Hideyoshi was in Kyoto with his army of battle-hardened samurai, and he inflicted a swift defeat on Akechi. During the following year, Hideyoshi made sure that the Oda clan's army and all the vassals were purged of all those who would oppose his supremacy as Nobunaga's successor.

After his leadership position was firmly established, Hideyoshi committed himself to finish what his master started.

Toyotomi Hideyoshi was quite an interesting character, too. Apart from being a bold, competent, and successful military leader, he also had an impressive backstory, at least by today's standards. Namely, thanks to Nobunaga's doctrine of running a meritocracy among his ranks, Hideyoshi, who was most likely of peasant ancestry, was able to climb to the very top of his master's forces.

Some two years after avenging Nobunaga's death and continuing his mission, Hideyoshi came into conflict with Tokugawa Ieyasu, a powerful clan leader who also possessed aspirations to take over the process of unification. The two clashed over a period roughly between 1584 and 1585, after which Tokugawa Ieyasu gave up his ambition, at least for the time being. While it was unclear at that time, Tokugawa was to become the last of the three great unifiers of the Azuchi-Momoyama period some years later, with the first two being Nobunaga and Hideyoshi, of course.

In the course of 1585, Hideyoshi managed to get many other things done, such as destroying all the remaining militant Buddhist opposition and claiming the island of Shikoku. Just two years later, all of Kyushu also fell under Hideyoshi's control, and he conducted a thorough lustration of the local daimyos, regardless of whether or not their claims there were legitimate, installing those who were loyal.

By the year 1591, Hideyoshi's conquests were a major success. With his massive army of samurai, he finally secured control over all of Honshu Island and even began to expand into Hokkaido, which was then known as "Ezochi," meaning "alien territory." This island was home to indigenous populations such as the Ainu, many of whom didn't take lightly to Yamato incursions. Hokkaido was far from conquered and, at this stage, the important thing was that Japan had at least some foothold on the island, on which further expansion could be built in the future. For the time being, the presence on Hokkaido was mostly relegated to outposts and smaller dominions in the southern part of the island.

Apart from just stringing along a bunch of military victories and slaughtering all of his enemies, Hideyoshi tended to many other important matters of state consolidation during his rule until 1598. Judging by the reforms he initiated, Hideyoshi most likely had two main goals: reducing the risk of future civil war or rebellion against him and severely curbing the power of the daimyos. For one, Hideyoshi started a country-wide disarmament program that targeted both swords and guns among farmers, religious sects, and other groups. He also imposed restrictions on the Christian missionaries in the country, who were becoming rather aggressive in their conversion efforts. On top of all this, Hideyoshi also banned people's ascension up the social classes and imposed taxes to fund the state.

Toyotomi Hideyoshi's long-standing dream was to conquer China, which he intended to do by taking Korea first. Operating a massive army and feeling emboldened by all of his successes, Hideyoshi embarked upon this crusade in 1592, but the Korean resistance, supported by many Chinese volunteers, was stiff. The failed invasion went on until 1598, after which Hideyoshi died.

Immediately after his death, succession became a hot topic. Although the late leader had a son by the name of Hideyori, the boy was too young to take over. To account for this issue in advance, Hideyoshi had no choice but to ask the daimyos in his inner circle to pledge loyalty to his son and rule only until he comes of age. The man of highest wealth and influence among these vassals, who had been patiently waiting for his opportunity to take over ever since 1585 was Tokugawa Ieyasu.

Toyotomi Hideyoshi, a preeminent daimyo, warrior, general and politician of the Sengoku period, his statue situated in front of Hokoku shrine

Tokugawa refused to honor Hideyoshi's request, quickly moved to establish his hegemony, and formed a government over the conquered and consolidated territory. The other daimyos, from within and without Hideyoshi's inner circle, became divided on the issue. Some supported the powerful Tokugawa and agreed to become his vassals, while others formed alliances to oppose his claim, either because of their own ambitions or their outrage over the undoing of Hideyoshi's will.

The country plunged into conflict once again, but Tokugawa and his allies proved too overpowering for their opposition, and the conflict only lasted two years, culminating with Tokugawa's crushing victory in the Battle of Sekigahara in 1600.

As was a tradition by this point, Tokugawa formed a military government and relocated it to a city, which was Edo in this case. In present-day Tokyo, Tokugawa established a Shogunate that would last close to three centuries and, like all Shoguns before him, he left the imperial court and all its offices in Kyoto untouched, so they could continue to play their religious and symbolic role. And so, the era of Medieval Japan came to an end, making way for the 17th century and Japan's entrance into the Modern Era.

Chapter 8: Edo – Japan Enters the Modern Era

After centuries of struggle and strife over power, Japan had finally been united and was ready to enter the Modern Era under its new military leadership. Ieyasu spent the first few years of his newly formed Shogunate smoothing things out for the long run and, much like his predecessors, purging his ranks. The first targets, in the immediate aftermath of his victory at Sekigahara, were almost ninety daimyos who allied themselves with the army that opposed him. The estates of these daimyos were simply confiscated and redistributed among those who were loyal to Ieyasu or transferred into his own property.

The Edo period is sometimes seen as having started in 1603 because this was the year when Ieyasu obtained the Emperor's official appointment to the Shogun office, which finalized the legitimacy of his Shogunate. In a symbolic move intended to send a message, Ieyasu stepped down just two years later and allowed his son Hidetada to succeed him as Shogun. By doing this, Ieyasu sought to solidify his Shogunate as successive along hereditary lines in the eyes of the country, but he maintained a tight hold on all affairs of state, of course.

Eleven years later in 1614, Ieyasu decided to put an end to the last remnant of the tumultuous Sengoku times – Hideyoshi's son, Hideyori. The boy was not killed during or after the decisive battle in 1600, and he had been living in his father's formidable castle in Osaka since then. Ieyasu worked on the siege of the castle during late 1614 and finally attacked in 1615, successfully tying up one last loose end.

Beyond these growing pains, the Edo period in Japan was generally a rather stable time during which a lot of progress was made in many regards. The Tokugawa Shogunate was strict, however, and this affected some more than others, but it ultimately was a stabilizing factor. The country was so stable for most of this period, in fact, that the samurai armies gradually became less than profitable, putting a strain on the economy. Edo was also a time of increased interaction with Europeans and isolationism at the same time.

Founded in 1617, the remains of Tokugawa Ieyasu
are entombed here at the Yomeimon gate.

Despite his betrayal of his predecessor's heir, Ieyasu continued to build upon some of the policies that were enacted by Hideyoshi. For one, he continued to suppress the influx of Christianity and persecuted Christians even more, starting around 1614. Ieyasu was also hard at work keeping the daimyos in check. Under the so-called alternate attendance system, daimyos was obliged to move to Edo every second year and spend that year in the proximity of the Shogun. By being kept away from his estates for so long, a daimyo would lose profits, but it would also be difficult for him to scheme, expand without authorization, and grow his power in general.

The balance of power seemed static with no trouble on the horizon. Because of this stability, Japan was able to focus on improving itself in important. Prolonged peace allowed the population to grow substantially and double in the first century of the Edo period, reaching up to 30,000,000. With no wars to fight, many people turned to reading and educating themselves, which increased literacy and produced more literature. In turn, the number of schools grew, and more people sought to involve themselves in various businesses. The government also invested in improving the country's infrastructure.

This time was also essential for the development of Japanese art, which was unprecedented during Edo, producing haiku poetry, kabuki theaters, and much else between the second half of the 17th and early 18th centuries. The famous ukiyo-e woodblock prints also became very popular, and they are now symbolic of Edo Japan for many who appreciate art and its history.

Early in the 17th century, however, the Shogunate gradually became somewhat wary of Western influence and started to move toward isolationism under Shogun Iemitsu in 1633. This shift was finalized by 1639 when the Shogunate officially initiated the Sakoku, or "closed country" policy.

Nikko Taiyuinbyo is the mausoleum of the third
Tokugawa shogun, Iemitsu, the grandson of Ieyasu

While foreigners, including Koreans and the Chinese, were prohibited from traveling to Japan under penalty of enslavement or death, trade with both China and the Netherlands was curbed but not entirely abolished. The government established a special port on Kyushu specifically designated for trade with the Dutch. Dutch merchants were expected to come to this trading post, conduct limited business with the Japanese in a monitored environment, and leave. This port later became the Nagasaki Port of today.

Travel was also forbidden for Japanese citizens who were not allowed to leave the country. Punishments for the Japanese who broke these laws were the same as for the foreigners. The government also banned foreign literature, although this ban was later lifted in 1720, as the country revised only some aspects of its isolationist policy.

Most importantly, the Japanese could now buy various scientific and engineering pieces of literature from the Dutch. By studying these books throughout the 18ᵗʰ century, the Japanese gained insight into various engineering feats of the Western civilization, but also geography, medicine and anatomy, chemistry, physics, and much else.

Japan was also consolidating its nation and beginning to work on strengthening a sense of nationalism during this time. The Shogunate sought to clearly categorize the Japanese society into four well-defined classes, including the samurai, who formed the very top of the pyramid, followed by peasants, artisans, and finally merchants. The Tokugawa Shogunate maintained Hideyoshi's ban on social ladder climbing as well. Steps were also taken to infuse a dose of nationalism into the education system.

Despite maintaining stability, the country began to stagnate in the late 18ᵗʰ century, particularly when it came to the economy. With stagnation, the samurai caste became an even greater economic burden. On top of that, natural disasters struck many areas throughout the period and, in combination with the raising of taxes in an effort to mend the government's financial troubles, the peasants found it increasingly difficult to survive. Famines and other issues gradually produced more discontent.

Japan's problems accelerated when more and more foreign powers, starting with Russia, kept coming to the country and requesting to set up trade relations. Japan repeatedly refused such proposals, much to the dismay of the foreigners. All of this perhaps contributed to a sense of urgency to change something, especially among those who were already getting fed up with the increasingly apparent deterioration of the country.

The insistence of foreign powers became dramatic in 1853 when Commodore Matthew Perry of the American Navy sailed in with a contingent of large, modern gunboats that far outmatched any naval power Japan could muster. The Commodore demanded that Japan open itself up to trade at the threat of attack. The Tokugawa Shogunate was utterly humiliated when Japan was forced to sign trade agreements that were deemed very unfair. Russia, the US, and the British Empire were allowed to come to Japan, move about freely, and conduct business without any real hindrance.

Chapter 9: The Meiji Restoration

In 1868, the Meiji Restoration, one of the most decisive periods of Japanese history, began. After almost seven centuries of nearly uninterrupted military dictatorship, Japan was finally about to restore imperial rule to the country. 1868 thus marked the beginning of the Meiji period, which would last until 1912. Much of the power was also transferred into the hands of nobles who assumed high positions in the military, some of whom had a samurai background.

The humiliation and outright violation of sovereignty that Japan suffered at the hands of Western colonial powers led to a lot of discontent and was the last straw for many clans and individuals alike. The legitimacy of the Shogunate came into question, ideas about restoring the power of the imperial court were being flown, and the people protested. The staunchest critics were the domains of Satsuma and Choshu, who hated Western subjugation of Asian powers and saw the Tokugawa's signing of the contract with them as the Shogunate essentially selling the country.

The dissatisfaction with the situation culminated in early 1868 when the two allied domains, with many supporting daimyos, finally decided to make their move and overthrow the Shogunate. This swift and successful coup is known as the Boshin War. Thus came the end of the 268-year rule by the Tokugawa Shogunate, and the changes that ensued were spectacular, giving birth to the Empire of Japan and making the country all but unrecognizable by 1912. Right after the victory over Tokugawa, the teenage Emperor Meiji, who had assumed the throne in 1867, was moved from Kyoto to Edo along with the imperial court, and the city was renamed as "the Eastern Capital," or Tokyo.

The long-term geopolitical ambition of the imperial government, which would shape Japan's path for decades to come, was to reassert Japan as a formidable force to be reckoned with and reclaim the country's pride. Seeing no end in sight to the colonial attempts to subjugate and exploit Japan, the Empire knew it had to develop the capability to project power beyond its main islands and simply deny the Western countries' free reigns in Asia with economic as well as military means.

The imperial government soon rooted out the last remnants of the old feudal structure by transferring the ownership of all daimyo assets to the Emperor,a swift process finalized by 1870. The former domains were restructured and reorganized, and Japan's administration was broken down into prefectures. Many other reforms followed, including the cessation of Christian persecution that marked the reign of the Shoguns, and the government granted religious freedom to its citizens as early as 1873, although the government declared Shintoism the official state faith.

Old mythical ideas of the Emperor's divine origin and the legendary descent of the eternal Imperial House of Japan from Heaven itself were brought back to the surface and infused with a renewed patronage of the Shinto faith and Confucian morality. The government then initiated education reforms, one of which was to make schooling compulsory. The goal was to elevate literacy to new heights, but schools were also now used to teach nationalism.

Despite the general perception toward the West, Japan understood that it would have to westernize if it were to become strong. Selective but massive westernization occurred for much of the Meiji period. In order to catch up to the West, Japan rapidly began to industrialize. To support this process, the country opened itself up to foreign experts but also sent its own talented individuals abroad to study and come back to Japan with valuable knowledge and expertise. Infrastructure was another area of major reform thanks to the construction of telegraph lines and the improvement of transportation.

The next major points of focus were, of course, the military and the government. Just like in industry, education, and infrastructure, Japan adopted Western models in these two sectors. First, funds were allocated to form a large, well-equipped, and, above all, modern military force and navy. Conscription was introduced to fill the ranks of the army. The structuring and organization of both the army and the navy were based on prominent European powers whose land armies and naval armadas were tried and true.

Western influence also influenced the government and the political system of the country. For instance, 1889 saw the introduction of the first constitution of Japan, much in line with those of modern European countries. While the Emperor maintained de jure control over the military and represented the executive and legislative branches of the government, Japan received its first parliament called the Diet, although political parties would come sometime later.

All the reforms brought about some financial trouble in the 1880s, which, in turn, led the leadership to implement even more reforms, particularly in the financial sector by establishing the Bank of Japan and reorganizing the currency system of the country. In the end, Japan was completely reborn to much surprise of many political analysts at the time. After all that Westernization, t Japan would follow the example of the colonial powers in more than one area.

The Wars

The next step that the Empire of Japan had to take in order to meet its goals was to expand. Japan wanted to possess many pieces of land in the Pacific and mainland Asia. These acquisitions were all strategic, necessary stepping stones in Japan's bid to assert its influence in the region. After settling some of the more immediate territorial questions early in the Meiji period, such as the northern Hokkaido Island, Japan set its gaze to the west and south. These policies ensured that Japan was bound to walk into a greater military confrontation, but the imperial government had confidence in the reforms it implemented within the military. The first major campaign was the enduring Japanese ambition of annexing Korea starting with the Japanese invasion of the peninsula in 1894. Of course, a land as close and as strategically important as the Korean Peninsula was bound to cause a conflict with neighboring China, and the first Sino-Japanese War began that same year. However, Japan subdued China in less than a year and seized Taiwan and many other territories including Korea. The Japanese forces went further into Manchuria, to the north and west of Korea, also occupying the Liaodong Peninsula.

The Western powers, on the other hand, were very displeased with Japan's aggressive expansion. Concerned about their own colonial interests in the region, France, Russia, and Germany forced Japan to give up Korea and some other lands but allowed Japan to keep

Taiwan. The period that followed, however, saw Korea remain in the Japanese sphere of influence despite a lack of military occupation.

The balance of power was shifting, and Korea was quickly turning into a flashpoint, particularly between Japan and Russia. Pursuing its eternal geopolitical mission of obtaining warm water ports, Russia was heavily invested in Manchuria. The Russians were building their south Manchuria railway that led into the Liaodong, and since Japan had already led an incursion into the area, the Russians significantly increased their forces there to prevent future issues and protect their railway project. Once the construction was completed, Russia moved even more troops into southern Manchuria, increasing tensions as Japan was still looking into ways of reclaiming its gains.

Seeing common ground with Japan in its desire to curb Russian influence, the British formed a military alliance with Japan in 1902. This alliance greatly strengthened Japan's resolve, and the imperial government went to war against Russia, essentially a superpower at that time, in 1904. Incredibly enough, Japan eventually came out on top in 1905, impressing the world. After making territorial gains in this war and showing its strength, Japan went on to annex Korea fully in 1910. Only two years later, Emperor Meiji died at age 59 and was succeeded by Taisho.

Chapter 10: Taisho

As Emperor Taisho came onto the scene in 1912, so did the period that bore his name. The initial days of Taisho's reign were ones of mourning by the deeply patriotic Japanese for the deceased, beloved Meiji. Indeed, by the time 1912 rolled around, the many reforms and efforts the government made to foster a sense of nationalism in the Japanese citizens were starting to pay off.

Through education, the media, religion, and other means, the government helped create a deep devotion and connection between the people and the country, especially the Emperor. After close to seven centuries of Shogun rule, the new government had managed, in a little over four decades, to make the Emperor not just loved but worshiped as a divine being.

Nationalism was only emboldened by the military successes against China and Russia under Meiji, and these glorious victories illustrated to the people that the reforms, hard work, and utmost devotion to the Emperor were worth the effort. The military accomplishments also demonstrated to the people that Japan was strong enough to secure a prosperous, influential future for itself in the region. An idea grew in the country that revolved around Japanese leadership in the Asian struggle to rid the region of European influence and subjugation.

Throughout the Taisho period this campaign of etching nationalism deep into the soul of the Japanese was still going strong. The government also used ancient texts and literature to bolster their propaganda, always putting an emphasis on the spiritual side of Japan. Over time, those who were thoroughly indoctrinated would come to believe in the divinity and holiness of the Japanese state itself, which gave way to feelings of immense superiority.

This period started off fairly well for the Empire of Japan and its expansionist ambitions, but a bumpy road lie ahead when the period ended in 1926 with the beginning of Hirohito's reign. Unfortunately, Emperor Taisho was characterized by many as a less than ideal ruler. Some believed he was weak and unable to amount to the legacy left behind by his father. On top of that, he suffered from health issues.

Whatever the truth may be, the emerging Empire of Japan needed more and more resources to fuel its formidable industry and grow the armed forces even further. Clearly, the Empire had to expand upon its gains, which were secured during the wars under Meiji. Japan was beginning to take aim at securing territories well beyond its home islands, such as the entire Chinese coast, the Philippines, the Dutch

East Indies in present-day Indonesia, and many smaller islands throughout the Pacific. Many important political changes and developments that seemed ominously reminiscent of Japan's old troubles occurred during the Taisho period. In the beginning, the power of the military nobles who exerted great influence during the Meiji period was being eroded. Certain steps would be taken to further democratize the country, but not everything worked out.

Before that time of politics, however, it was a time of war, at least as far as Europe was concerned. Just two years into Taisho's reign, Europe and many other places in the world were plunged into the Great War.

World War I

Imperial rivalries and paranoia between the great European powers were culminating toward 1914, but the peripheral locales on the Old Continent had been unstable and tense for years beforehand. After a series of unfortunate events and diplomatic catastrophes, Europe was quickly descending into war. On its way to France, Germany violated Belgium's neutrality, which triggered a reaction from Britain immediately.

Japan was still in an alliance with Britain, so it became invested in the war very quickly. The Japanese military wouldn't see much fighting during this war, however, and the Empire's role against the Central Powers consisted of a combination of logistical support to allies like Britain and opportunism. While Germany was preoccupied with the war in Europe, Japan, in coordination with the British, proceeded to absorb many German-held islands south of the home islands. They did the same to German assets in northeastern China. In exchange for the support, Japan sent logistic assistance to the British in Europe.

Even before taking German colonies, Japan was presented with a viable business opportunity as soon as the Great War began. Japan put its industry into high gear to churn out various products that would be needed in many parts of the world during the war, including different kinds of weaponry. Not only was Japan producing valuable supplies, but it also had the capability of shipping them to various destinations.

Japan got even more aggressive in its expansionist policies toward China. Before long, the Empire of Japan sent demands to the Chinese. Weakened by their problems, the Chinese had no real way of fighting back against the emerging regional superpower Japan had become, and Western powers were otherwise preoccupied. Japan soon obtained significant influence over China's economic and political matters. After a while, Japanese forces began to run into resistance groups in colonized parts of Chinese and Korean lands, to which they responded with brutal crackdowns.

And while Europe was embroiled in its calamity, none of Japan's moves went unnoticed by the watchful eye of the US, especially when Japan edged eastward in the Pacific. Besides, Japan's eyeing of the Philippines was especially worrisome, as the Philippines were colonized by the US. As such, America had its own ambitions in this theater at the time, and it was all too clear to Washington what Japan was up to. Soon, the two powers became rivals, both on their own imperial missions in the Pacific Ocean.

After the Great War

After World War I came to an end, Japan was even allowed to participate in the Paris Peace Conference of 1919, where the allied, victorious nations deliberated over the various peace terms associated with the defeated Central Power as well as the future steps to take to prevent anything like the Great War happening again. The Treaty of Versailles emerged as a result as did the recognition of Japanese colonial gains in the East. Japan's role in the conference wasn't merely symbolic either, as the country was included in the five major powers, right alongside the US, Italy, France, and Britain, and joined the newly established League of Nations.

Despite receiving recognition of its new colonies, Japan was dealt a significant blow during this conference. Namely, the Empire of Japan proposed an amendment to the racial equality clause of the Covenant of the League of Nations, which would guarantee equal treatment of other races in the legal and every other sense. Britain, the US, and Australia shot down this proposal, which cut a deep divide between Japan and the Western powers, reminiscent of the time when Japan was humiliated by American naval forces during the late Edo period. Policies of racial discrimination would culminate in 1924, when the US Congress passed the Exclusion Act, implementing a ban on all immigration from Japan.

As if Japan's expansionism and imperial ambition weren't enough, quarrels like these pushed Japan even further away from the West and emboldened and justified ultra-nationalism in the country. After the major gains during the war, the Japanese economy also began to decline as the 1920s were underway.

The 1920s were a time of many political innovations, changes, and tensions. This period saw the introduction of party politics in Japan, which gave rise to a liberalization process and the emergence of many new political movements with various locations on the political spectrum. The people were empowered to engage in the political process of the country, which was improved when all male citizens over the age of 25 were given voting rights in 1925. Nationalism and internationalism were perhaps the two primary opposing wings of the Japanese political discourse, which emerged thanks to these reforms.

However, the struggle between different power structures also became apparent, and certain influencers who were very nationalistic and militaristic saw the liberalization of politics as a major weakness and threat to Japan. Political divisions, exacerbated by economic problems, gave rise to a very tense sociopolitical climate in the country.

The horrific Great Kanto Earthquake of 1923, which struck the Kanto plain and ravaged the capital Tokyo as well as Yokohama and many settlements in the vicinity, also contributed to the grim outlook. Up to 140,000 souls perished in this catastrophe, caused directly by the earthquake or indirectly through the fires and other misfortunes as a result of the quake. The earthquake caused devastation in the economic sense as well, in addition to being overall demoralizing.

All of these misfortunes lead to a significant amount of instability, and the Emperor seemed hardly capable of remedying the country's problems. His influence diminished. Many high ranking officials and nobles surrounding him had their own ideas of where the country should go, and many of them were those same nationalistic, militaristic cadres that lurked in the corridors of power the entire time. In a bid to pull the country together and maintain stability, the Peace Preservation Act was passed in 1925, which significantly curbed civil liberties. In a time where political disagreements were cropping up and workers were going on strikes, this act now made it illegal to participate in or incite any form of social unrest. The punishments were severe, and the criteria for what would be deemed as "social unrest" by the authorities was open to being abused and manipulated to facilitate crackdowns on dissent.

The imperial ambitions and expansionist foreign policy were here to stay, and the military elites would not let economic issues or political liberties get in the way of this agenda. By this point, Japan's ghosts of the past seemed to have been looming over the country's destiny once again, as militarism gained momentum. Emperor Taisho died somewhat prematurely in 1926 and was succeeded by Hirohito, inheriting a proper mess.

Chapter 11: Showa

Showa, roughly translated as the "Period of Enlightened Peace," was a decisive period in the history of modern Japan corresponding to the reign of Emperor Hirohito between 1926 and 1989. Due to the magnitude and impact of the events that transpired in this relatively short time, the period is usually divided into prewar Showa, post-war occupation, and post-occupation Showa. The name of this period was perhaps tragically ironic, as a considerable portion of Showa included some of the darkest moments of Japanese history and wreaked unspeakable havoc on the people of Japan and the entire region, not to mention the world as a whole, engulfed in the flames of World War II.

Enlightened peace was simply not to be, as Japan's path through the pre-1945 years of Showa was mostly set under Taisho, although the seeds were planted even earlier. Either way, Hirohito inherited a country with quite a few problems. The consequences of the horrific Kanto earthquake were still being felt, and they put a strain on the economy as well as the spirit of many. When the peak of the Great Depression's impact on Japan hit in 1929, things only got worse.

By that time, the Empire of Japan relied heavily on foreign trade. As a good part of the global economy came tumbling down, many of Japan's trade partners had domestic, economic issues so grave that they just couldn't afford to buy goods from other countries anymore. As a result, Japan lost devastating amounts of its profits, ultimately affecting wages in the country as well.

The ensuing decade in the 1930s can be viewed as a well-documented, modern example of the gradual erosion of Japanese imperial authority and the rise of the military elites. Even though Japan was under the leadership of Shogunate for many centuries, the affairs of long-past eras seem somewhat distant. Seeing as the Showa period had the best written records up to that point, cameras, and much else, the proximity of these events to our modern comprehension truly unveils a full spectrum of horror that can be unleashed by a military dictatorship.

The difference, however, is in post-restoration Japan, notably in the Meiji constitution, Emperors had concrete, de jure powers that they could legally employ. The events that ensued, particularly the Emperor's responsibility for them, are so hotly debated to this day.

The Second Sino-Japanese War

As far as the West is concerned, when we think back on the period of destruction around World War II, most of us refer to either the year 1939 or 1941 in our minds. Unfortunately, the Japanese people don't have that luxury. For the Empire of Japan, a state of perpetually escalating conflict began as early as 1931, leading to wars that would overlap and occur side by side with Japan's involvement in World War II until the war's gruesome conclusion in 1945.

War ascended on the horizon in 1931, with the occurrence of the Manchurian incident, also known as Mukden. This event happened when the Japanese Kwantung Army, which was stationed and in charge of maintaining Japanese authority in Korea and adjacent colonies, launched a full-scale invasion of the entire Manchuria on a fabricated pretext. The Kwantung Army's job was also to protect the Japanese settlers and infrastructure in those parts, including railroads, factories, and the like. The army had been itching to march on China for a long time, so it decided to stage a false flag, a bombing attack on one of the Japanese railroads. Operating on a mere assumption that the authorities in Tokyo would fully support it, the Kwantung Army launched an offensive immediately, quickly sweeping through Manchuria and captured all of northeast China as well as parts of Mongolia. The truth is that the court knew of the scheme before it even happened but chose to ignore the warning. And when the invasion was complete and successful, nobody was arrested for insubordination or rogue conduct – Japan simply incorporated the new territories.

Manchuria was given a status of an "independent state" with a Chinese "Emperor," but this was essentially a puppet regime for the Japanese armies. Japan was strongly condemned by the League of Nations for the actions of its armed forces, but Japan simply left the organization by 1933 and continued its campaigns, much to Hirohito's dismay.

Through to 1936, Japan would gradually take more and more Chinese territories either by coercing the leaders into treaties or by brute force. Tokyo remained on the sidelines, and the Emperor was apparently powerless to put a leash on his forces. Possibly, Hirohito feared that if he stood up to the army, he would be killed. This year, different factions in China began to see Japan as the existential threat, and they began working together in growing numbers, mounting a resistance.

Seeing this consolidation among the thus-far balkanized Chinese, Japanese military leadership was determined to nip it in the bud before it became a serious threat. In July, a full-scale war was set in motion, beginning with the devastating bombing and assault on Shanghai. The Battle of Shanghai was the first major engagement of the Second Sino-Japanese War, wreaking havoc on the city and its people, the defenders, but also on the invading Japanese forces.

Clearly, this excruciating conflict was fueled by notions of superiority, ultra-nationalism, and rabid militarism with a hatred which ran deep. By the end of the year, the Japanese forces seized the capital of Nanking. Here, the hatred would culminate in a shocking six-week-long campaign of rape, massacre, looting, and destruction that would leave between 90,000-300,000 residents dead. The Second Sino-Japanese war would continue for over eight years until the total and utter defeat of Japan.

World War II

By 1940, Japan had done away with the Western powers, the League of Nations, and essentially any authority other than the divine rule of the Emperor. During that year, common interests were identified between the Empire of Japan, Nazi Germany, and Mussolini's Italy, and the Tripartite Pact was signed, forming the Axis. Also, after a brief border skirmish with the Soviets to the north, the two countries signed a non-aggression pact.

Japan could now focus on its troubles in China and on fulfilling other imperial ambitions in the Pacific. Seeing as France had been incapacitated and Britain was under heavy pressure by the German air raids, Japan almost had free-reign over the west Pacific to seize many valuable colonial assets in Indochina, Indonesia (Dutch East Indies), and elsewhere. These colonies would have been conquered swiftly and painlessly, but the only problem in the equation was the United States. Japan and its war machine depended heavily on American oil, and moving further into the French Indochina ran the risk of angering the US. An alternative was to seize Indonesia for its oil reserves, in which case America would likely respond militarily.

This position was unfavorable for Japan, and the US was fully aware. Starting around 1940, American pressure reached new heights when Franklin D. Roosevelt started demanding that Japan begin withdrawing from China or face an oil embargo. After years of war and hundreds of thousands of fallen soldiers, to just quit and go home was out of the question for Japan, and the US soon began applying the pressure.

Some of the military leadership in Japan began to think that a swift and devastating attack to neutralize the US Navy's Pacific Fleet was the only option to ensure Japan's security in the Pacific. And thus, on December 7, 1941, at the instruction of Japanese leaders headed by Prime Minister Tojo Hideki, the Empire of Japan struck the US Navy at Pearl Harbor, Hawaii. The goal was to neutralize America's capacity to wage war in the Pacific, so Japan could proceed into Brunei and seize Dutch oil, breaking its dependence on US exports. This attack was the culmination of a rivalry stretching back to the middle of the Great War.

The ensuing four-year war started rather well for the Japanese, but after the Battle of Midway in June of 1942, the tide gradually turned against Japan, and it never really turned back around. For the remainder of the war, Japan was mostly on the defense in the Pacific Theater. America also had other allies in the theater, such as the British and the Australians, who were attacked and threatened quite a few times by the Japanese.

After the Guadalcanal Campaign and a string of other successes, the Americans encroached ever closer on strategically crucial Japanese islands, constantly increasing the pressure on mainland Japan. Japan suffered prolonged, intense bombing campaigns, which inflicted enormous damage on the majority of its important cities, with the exception of Kyoto. Notably, the persistent firebombing of Tokyo, resulted in upward of 100,000 deaths.

In 1945, after defeating Japan in the excruciating but decisive battles of Iwo Jima and then Okinawa, as part of the Volcano and Ryukyu Islands campaign, plans were being made to wrap up the war. The Japanese soldiers, who fought with unfathomable devotion to their Emperor and country, showed at bloody Okinawa that the closer Americans came to mainland Japan the more corpses they would be forced to bury. In a bid to avoid prolonging the war indefinitely and to minimize further casualties, the US employed atomic weapons against the Japanese cities of Hiroshima and Nagasaki on August 6 and 9. The attacks killed around 200,000 people, mostly civilians.

Neither this attack nor the encroaching Soviets in Manchuria were enough to convince some of the military leaders to surrender, which was an offer they received many times prior to the atomic attacks. Finally, Emperor Hirohito decided to stand up and use his constitutional and *divine* right to act. The Emperor accepted and signed the surrender of Japan on August 14 unconditionally.

Genbaku Dome, the ruins of the atomic bombing of Hiroshima in 1945.
It sits 150m from the blast centre.

Post-War and Post-Occupation Japan

Japan fell under American occupation and governance soon after surrendering and remained as such until 1952. The first commander of the occupation was the distinguished General Douglas MacArthur, who was replaced by General Matthew Ridgway for the final year of the operation.

Japan was in an abysmal state after the war and needed strong and competent leadership with a long-term plan if it were to ever reemerge out of its nightmare. A part of that plan was the adoption of the so-called Yoshida Doctrine under one of the first post-war Prime Ministers, Shigeru Yoshida. Japan would focus every effort and every atom of its being on total economic recovery and rebirth while the security needs of the country would be provided for by the US.

Right after occupation, Japan also lost the territorial gains made after 1894. Lands were ceded to the USSR, China, and, temporarily, to the US. The Americans de facto annexed Okinawa and most of the Ryukyu Islands until 1972 when they were returned to Japanese administration and sovereignty, but the American military presence remains on Okinawa to this day.

Once again, the Emperor had been relegated to a little more than a figurehead and symbol of the country by the constitution of 1947. The constitution gave the Japanese were given voting rights across the board, and the country was heavily democratized and secularized. Of course, human rights, as they are generally applied in Western countries, were also established and guaranteed by the constitution.

Article 9 of the constitution strictly forbade Japan from ever using war in any shape or form as a means of settling any issues in foreign policy, also abolishing the armed forces, with an understanding that Japan was not to maintain an army anymore. Accordingly, what was left of the Japanese military was destroyed.

Finally, war crime trials were also held, seeing many generals, politicians, and lower-ranking perpetrators put to death for their crimes. Emperor Hirohito, however, was not tried, as he was determined by the US and the tribunal to have not been in charge. This decision was heavily contested by critics, who pointed to the powers granted to the Emperor by the Meiji Constitution, including the position as supreme commander of the military. Either way, the decision stood, and the Emperor was allowed to complete his reign in peace. After the occupation ended in 1952, Japan entered another important sub-period of its history.

As the Cold War gained intensity and the war in Korea erupted in 1950, the US insisted Japan form a sort of military, due to fears that communists might take root in the country and cause instability. After the Peace Treaty was signed in 1952 and the occupation ended, the US and Japan still maintained strong security ties, and the US continued to exert influence. Finally, in 1954, the highly controversial decision to form the Japanese Self Defense Forces was made. Although the JSDF was envisioned as a strictly defensive organization, the debate over its legitimacy persists to this day, as do the strong military ties with America.

Two years later, Japan joined the UN and retook its position in the international community, although with a much different outlook. Japan always advocated strongly for peace and has always been especially vocal against nuclear proliferation. Over time, some wounds were healed, and Japan managed to reestablish relations with China and normalize them in 1972, which was also the year Japan got its islands back from the US.

Emperor Showa's tomb in Hachioji, Japan. Emperor Showa also called Hirohito was the father of the present Japanese emperor, Akihito.

In the period between the 1960s and 1980s, Japan's Yoshida Doctrine quickly came to fruition, and the economy grew exponentially, including industry and many other areas. Japan performed what some referred to as an economic miracle. Apart from the temporary oil crisis in 1973, which affected the country somewhat due to its dependence on foreign oil imports, most of post-occupation Showa saw incredible growth and recovery from the hell that were the war years. Emperor Hirohito passed away in 1989, leaving some in grief while reigniting hot topics with others.

Chapter 12: The Heisei Contemporary Japan

With the death of Hirohito Showa, as he was posthumously named, and the ascension of the current Japanese Emperor Akihito to the throne, Japan officially entered the ongoing Heisei period in 1989. Even in a short time span, several important things have happened and continue to happen. Japan's extensive post-war reforms are now largely complete, and the construction of a modern, democratic society has been consolidated.

Japan may no longer prowl the Pacific Ocean with formidable battleships and aircraft carriers, but in the short time since the allied occupation ended, Japan has certainly become an economic powerhouse, thanks to the miraculous economic recovery in the late Showa period. As Heisei came around, however, economic growth slowed down, and Japan went through some financial turmoil in the 1990s.

This economic stagnation was combined with and exacerbated by political instability. In the first couple of decades of the period, Japan saw more than fifteen Prime Ministers. This turnover reflected poorly on the country's direction due to unstable and inconsistent politics, including economic policies. To make matters worse, Japan's stock market was in quite a bubble around the beginning of the Heisei period, and sure enough, that bubble burst very quickly after 1989, crashing the market's value by around two thirds.

By this time, however, Japan's economy may have just been too big to fail. The issues were considerable, but not much changed in the way of living standards, and most people were much more concerned with the country's apparent inability to establish stable, competent leadership and set itself on a solid course. Japan finally achieved political stability when Prime Minister Shinzo Abe assumed office in 2012. Still, other issues were and continue to be a factor, and some of them are beyond Japan's control.

Recently, Japan appears to have entered something of a heated national debate when it comes to the assertion of Japan's regional, geopolitical position and the role the military might have in the future. The Japanese Self-Defense Forces have de facto come a long way toward being a formidable, national military force despite the imposed constitutional limits. Therefore, the ability of Japan's armed forces to engage in international conflicts now only lacks formal acknowledgment, as the military is more than capable of fulfilling such tasks. Japan's military operates a sizable, well-equipped, and well-trained land-based branch as well as an effective air force that fields numerous modern aircraft. As procurements gain momentum, the inventory grows larger and more sophisticated. Just as importantly, Japan's maritime military capabilities are growing exponentially due to an already large navy that is poised to become even bigger.

All of this has sparked fears of a resurgent militarization of Japan, which triggers dark memories from the recent past in the minds of many critics. At the same time, undeniable and legitimate security concerns have cropped up in East Asia over North Korea's nuclear program and fiery war rhetoric, which has emboldened the proponents of the Japanese military power and swayed public opinion in their favor. What's more important is that the current government under Prime Minister Shinzo Abe also seems to be in favor.

China's impending regional supremacy is another potential geopolitical challenge. Despite its economic strength and industry, Japan still depends heavily on certain imports, particularly oil. As such, it would perhaps be risky for Japan to leave itself at the mercy of other regional players who seek to put as many trading routes as possible under their control. This is another one of the reasons why Japan might want to reassert itself as a regional influencer in the near future, and it's a very solid reason too.

Unfortunately, the Heisei period brought other, much more immediate problems that were completely out of Japan's control, and those were natural disasters, among other things. On January 17, 1995, Japan's Kobe area was devastated by a major earthquake that left some 6,000 people dead and caused hundreds of billions of dollars in damage. In a way, this earthquake was also connected to the infamous sarin gas attack on the Tokyo subway on March 20 of that same year.

This attack was perpetrated by members of a doomsday cult called Aum Shinrikyo under the leadership of its founder, Asahara Shoko.

Among other things, this cult believed the Kobe earthquake was evidence of foreign schemes against Japan, a sign of impending doom. In Asahara's mind, the killing of "sinners" was justified, and he decided on the coordinated nerve agent attack on the Tokyo subway.

This attack wouldn't be the first time that the Aum Shinrikyo cult used sarin gas in attempted murders, and the cult was also connected to previous murders of the cult leader's critics. Seeing as how devastating and dangerous sarin gas is, it was a miracle in tragedy the attack killed only twelve people, but thousands were injured. The attacks shocked the world and showed how dangerous cult behavior can be. Asahara was later executed for his crimes, but, shockingly, the cult continues to exist and some of its original members remained in the ranks even after the attack.

Japan has also had problems of a more chronic nature in its recent history, and some of these issues persist with seemingly no end in sight. Perhaps the most discussed and debated problem associated with Japan is its demographic crisis. The country's population is aging, and the Japanese have a now infamously low, unsustainable birthrate.

For one, this issue has sparked fears of a shrinking workforce that could pose a serious threat to Japan's economy in the future.

Secondly, Japan has the highest life expectancy in the world, which is a good thing and a sign of a developed, well-functioning country, but when high life expectancy and an increase in the population's median age are coupled with a shrinking workforce, this discrepancy can put a significant strain on any country's economy.

The demographic crisis is an issue that mostly stems from significant social changes that have occurred in Japan after World War II. For most of its history, Japan has been a rather patriarchal society with very clearly defined gender roles. Women were expected to be homemakers and raise children while a man's job was to get an education and be the breadwinner. Toward the second half of the 20th century, however, the same expectation started to be put on women as was previously held by men, except that they were still supposed to address all of the needs of the household as well. This workload proved to be too much for many of them, so more and more women were getting married at a later age or not at all, choosing instead to solely pursue their professional ambitions. This shift was probably not the sole factor, but it coincided with an economic boom, and the situation is rather similar to a few other Asian countries, particularly South Korea, which has also seen immense economic growth.

Because of all this, Japan hasn't seen all sunshine and rainbows since 1989, but to say that the country is in some great distress or peril would be a serious misinterpretation of the facts. Japan is without a

118

doubt miles ahead of many if not most countries in the world in many crucial fields such as technology, infrastructure, health care, literacy, and many other factors that make it a well-organized, developed country.

Japan has also turned into an incredibly safe country. Violent crime, especially homicide, is truly a rarity with only 362 murders recorded in 2006, which amounts to a per-capita murder rate of 0.28 for every 100,000 citizens. In comparison, the homicide rate in the United States for that same year was 5.35. All manner of homicide is rare in Japan, but that is especially the case with gun violence, which is simply a freak occurrence in the country. Japan is, in most respects, a very good place to be nowadays despite a few general issues that really don't do much to hinder the life of the individual. For the most part, Japan may be facing the future with some uncertainty due to its demographic hardships and some potential threats in the region, but these issues can hardly compare with many of the adversities that the Japanese people have already surmounted in the past.

Despite the many social changes that have been taking place, some of which brought problems with them, the Japanese are still largely true to their traditions and values. The only problem is that this tide of changes has often clashed with the traditional Japanese way of life. As such, Japan seems to be in something of a limbo at times, which can cause stagnation, but this too is something that the Japanese have been through before. Japan is certainly here to stay and prosper, and any uncertainty that might exist at this time could well be just a prelude to a new era of growth, drastic change, and further evolution of the Japanese society.

Conclusion

Now that you have introduced yourself to the entirety of Japanese history, you have taken a giant leap toward gaining a deeper understanding of this fascinating, sometimes bewildering country in the Far East. As you can see, history is quite a teacher and can explain much about the current reality. Japanese culture and society contain famous yet misunderstood or seemingly inexplicable aspects, but the tale just told has hopefully shown you the root of some of the cultural aspects that are unique to Japan.

The student of Japanese history will also usually notice some recurring themes that permeate all those centuries, such as the seemingly eternal struggle between imperial and military authority, which seems to have left a deep mark on many of Japan's eras. Most countries have at least one sociopolitical factor or issue that seems to just follow them around forever. That one, deep-seated issue has a way of impacting or outright shaping many facets of a country's culture and society, and perhaps that's true in Japan's case as well.

All in all, Japan is certainly deserving of the hype surrounding it in Western popular culture these days, and the interest is more than justified. There We can learn so much about Japanese history that no one book could ever fully do it justice, but a mind thirsty for knowledge will always find a way to learn and, most importantly, to understand.

Bonus

As a way of saying thanks for your purchase, we're offering a special gift that's exclusive to my readers.

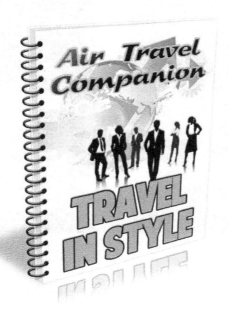

Visit this link below to claim your bonus.

http://dingopublishing.com/bonus/

More books from us

Visit our bookstore at: http://www.dingopublishing.com

Below is some of our favorite books:

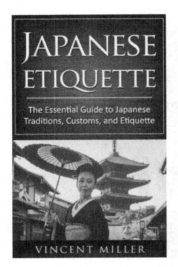 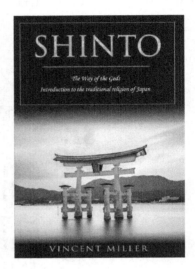

SIMPLE, HEALTHY AND DELICIOUS CHIA SEED RECIPES TO LIVE LONGER AND FEEL YOUNGER

CHIA SEEDS
Cookbook
Superfoods Every Day

Olivia Green

THE TOP 99 DELICIOUS RECIPES TO FIGHT CANCER AND RESTORE YOUR HEALTH

ANTI-CANCER
Diet

Olivia Green

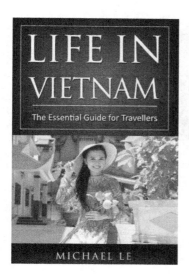

LIFE IN VIETNAM
The Essential Guide for Travellers

MICHAEL LE

RAMEN
NOODLES COOKBOOK
The Top 50 Delicious Ramen Recipes To Cook At Home

LINDA NGUYEN

Book excerpts: Japanese Etiquette

The essential guide to Japanese traditions, customs, and etiquette

By: Vincent Miller

Chapter 1: The Use of Names

One of the most important elements of Japanese etiquette is to be aware of how to address people and how to use names in different social and business settings.

Addressing People with Respect

San is a commonly used respectful expression that is put at the end of people's names while addressing them. San can be used when using the first name or the last name of the concerned individual. Also, san is used for all people irrespective of marital status or gender.

Sama is a term that is more appropriate in a formal setting and is to be used after the family name. Also, you must remember that you must use san or sama after everyone else's name (whom you wish to show respect to) but not after your own name. Here are some examples of the use of san and sama:

- Smith-san (Mr. Smith)
- Michael-san (Mr. Michael)

127

- Sandra-san (Ms. Sandra)
- Smith-sama (Mr. Smith again but to be used in a formal setting only)
- Tanaka-sama (Ms. Tanaka)

Another way of respectful address is by using the job title of the person along with his or her name. This works in a scenario where you need to address your superior at work or your teacher at school. For example, you can say Brown-sensei (Brown teacher; sensei is teacher in Japanese) instead of saying Brown-sama. Or bucho-san which is referring to your department head; bucho is head in Japanese.

In business environments, using surname instead of given or first name is more respectful. Use of one's job title instead of their name is also well accepted in Japanese business circles. This subtlety of using surnames instead of first names might come across as a bit stiff for some non-Japanese. However, you must remember that most Japanese are uncomfortable using first names.

However, there are a few Japanese citizens with a lot of exposure to Western cultures that have come to accept being addressed by their first names. Some of them have taken this even further and have created nicknames for themselves, which they embrace happily. You can use these nicknames too along with san or sama depending on the level of formality of the setting.

The final tip here is to remember that you can never go wrong using the surname with the san or sama suffix. For all else, it would be prudent to ask around and then make a sensible choice of addressing the concerned person. The convenience of san cannot be underestimated considering that it is unisex and, therefore, you don't have to worry about how to address people through email especially if the Japanese names are not clearly gender-specific.

Also, if someone is addressing you with the san suffix, accept it as a compliment. That's the intention of the Japanese name-calling etiquette.

Addressing Family and Friends

In Japan, addressing family members and friends also calls for politeness and respect though there is less formality than the use of san or sama. There is a plain form and there is a polite form when it comes to addressing family and friends. Here are a few examples:

- Otto or goshujin – husband
- Tsuma or okusan - wife
- Okoson – child in a polite form and Kodomo – child in a plain form
- Otosan – father in a polite form and Chichi – father in a plain form
- Okāsan – mother in a polite form and haha – mother in a plain form
- musukosan – son in a polite form and musuko – son in a plain form
- musumesan – daughter in a polite form and musume – daughter in a plain form
- otōtosan – older brother in a polite form and ani – older brother in a plain form
- onēsan – older sister in a polite form and ane – older sister in a plain form
- imōtosa – younger sister in a polite form and imōto – younger sister in a plain form
- tomodachi – friend

During conversations, shujin is used to refer to one's own husband and otto is used to refer to someone else's husband. Tsuma is used to refer to one's own wife and kanai is used to refer to someone else's wife

Here's the trick when it comes to using the plain form or the polite form. If you are addressing an older member of the family, then you must use the polite form. When addressing the younger members of the family (spouse also comes in the category), you can use the plain form. To get this right, you must also know the difference between referring to someone and addressing someone.

Referring to someone means you are not talking to the person but are referring to him or her in a conversation with someone else. Addressing someone, on the other hand, is talking to the person directly.

Commonly Used Japanese Expressions

While we are at this, let me also give you the top five commonly used expressions in Japanese conversations:

Yatta – I did it! – You can use this term whenever you have accomplished or been offered a great job or have won something. All these occasions can be classified under the 'Yatta' category.

Honto – Really? – This expression is used to let the person speaking to you know that you are listening to what is being said.

Â, SÔ DESU KA – I see – Also, a conversational bit of phraseology letting your partner (the one who is talking to you) know you are getting what is being said. A nod invariably accompanies this expression.

Mochiron – of course! – An expression of confidence

Zenzen – not at all – a phrase of emphatic denial (in a polite way) used for situations such as when someone asks you, "Am I disturbing you?" and you politely say, "zenzen."

Chapter 2: Greetings and Body Language Etiquette

There are many ways of greeting people when you meet them. This chapter is dedicated to these Japanese greeting methods.

Bowing

Bowing, or bending at the waist level, is a form of appreciation and respect shown by the person who is bowing to the person who is being bowed to. Bowing is a common form of greeting used along with:

- Good morning - ohayo gozaimasu
- Hello, good afternoon - konnichi wa
- With words of apology or gratitude (arigato)

There are three types of bows depending on how deep the waist is bent. These three types include:

The casual bow (eshaku bow)

Bending at a 15-degree angle, the casual bow also entails a slight tipping of the head. The eshaku bow is used when casual greetings are passed between people or when you pass someone belonging to a higher social status. Casual greetings in the form of good morning or good afternoon or thank you are sufficient by themselves. Yet, when used along with the eshaku bow makes the greeting more heartfelt.

The business bow (keirei bow)

This bow entails bending your torso at 30 degrees and is used when entering and/or leaving a meeting or conference or while greeting customers.

Deep bow (saikeirei bow)

This is the politest form of bowing in Japan and entails lowering the torso by 45 degrees. It is used to express very deep feelings of regret (apology) or gratitude.

Clasping Hands (Gassho)

Bringing both the palms together and clasping them in front of the chest is referred to as gassho. This form of greeting has its origins in Buddhism. Today, it is used before starting a meal and after finishing the meal along with the word, 'itadakimasu.' The word, 'itadakimasu,' means to receive or to accept an item or gift. It expresses gratitude for the food and for the person(s) who prepared the meal.

Bye-Bye

While 'sayonara' is the Japanese word for saying goodbye, the phrase 'bye-bye;' is also commonly used in the country. There is a subtle difference in the way the hand gesture works with sayonara. While in the West, you would open and close your palm as you lift your hand, in Japan, your open palms are waved from left to right and back. The hand is lifted high above your head so that the other person can see it and then the open palms are waved from left to right and back in a broad arch. The eshaku bow is also used commonly while saying bye-bye.

Shaking Hands

Although bowing is the more appropriate Japanese form of greeting, the handshake has come to be an accepted form of greeting, especially in a business setting. However, it is important to note that the handshake of the Japanese is far limper than the 'firm handshake' of the Western culture. This is easy to understand considering that the Japanese culture does not allow for too much physical contact, especially in public.

Body Language Etiquette

Nodding is an important gesture in Japan. When you are talking to someone, it is important that you nod often to imply comprehension. Your nod is telling the speaker that you are listening to him or her, and you are understanding what the person is trying to say.

Silence is an accepted form of nonverbal communication. There is no need to chatter merely to keep a conversation going. Silence is, in fact, an expected means of communication. Talk only when addressed or when it is your turn to do so.

Standing very close to a Japanese person is considered rude and uncomfortable. Avoid touching as much as possible except for that first handshake (the bow is a better option).

Making prolonged eye contact when talking to someone is also considered rude in Japanese culture.

Hugging, shoulder slapping, and other forms of physical contact are also to be avoided, especially in public. The Japanese frown on any outward show of affection of any kind.

Using your forefinger to beckon is disallowed. The Japanese way of beckoning calls for extending your right arm and bending the wrist in the downward direction. You are not allowed to beckon any person older than or senior to you.

How to Sit Correctly

Sitting in Japanese style calls for sitting on the floor and in an upright position. Even meals are had while sitting on the floor with low tables for the food. For tea ceremonies, it is mandatory to sit on the floor.

Both genders use the kneeling, or the seiza, posture to sit in a formal environment. It can get uncomfortable after some time for people (especially Westerners) who are not used to this way of sitting. In modern times, foreigners are exempted from sitting on the floor. In fact, many modern Japanese also find it difficult to sit like this for long. In casual environments, it is common to see men sitting cross-legged and women sitting with both their legs to one side.

If you are sitting on a chair, you are expected to sit with both your feet firmly placed on the ground. You cannot cross your legs or place your ankle on the knee while sitting on the chair.

The seating order works something like this: the most important person (usually the customer or the guest) is furthest away from the door. The place that is farthest away from the door is considered to be the good side in Japanese culture.

If there is a tokonoma (an alcove decorated with a hanging scroll accompanied by a flower arrangement), then the guest is usually placed in front of it. The least important person or the host takes the place closest to the door.

Also, in a business environment, all the people from the same company are seated on the same side of the table. When you visit Japanese businesses, it is common for the receptionist to show you your seat. If you don't see this happening, it might be prudent to ask before taking a seat.

**************** End of sample chapters ****************

Thanks again for purchasing this book.

We hope you enjoy it

Don't forget to claim your free bonus:

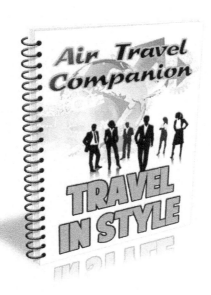

Visit this link below to claim your bonus now:

http://dingopublishing.com/bonus/

www.dingopublishing.com